DOMINOES

Five-up and Other Games
Including Official Rules and Odds

By DOMINIC C. ARMANINO

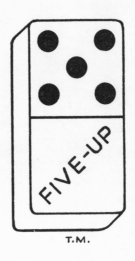

T.M.

DAVID McKAY COMPANY, INC.
New York

DOMINOES

First Paperback Edition, 1972
Reprinted August 1973
Reprinted April 1975

ISBN: 0-679-14009-3

Library of Congress Catalogue Card Number: 59-12264
Manufactured in the United States of America

Dedicated to the ever-fun-loving sports-
men. The Lord must love them—He
made so many and endowed them with
the lofty ideals of sportsmanship.

DOM ARMANINO

Acknowledgments

I want to express here my appreciation to my friend, Vaden R. Mayers, head of Mathematics Department, San Mateo High School, San Mateo, California, for his excellent work with the mathematics in the games of dominoes and his help in preparing and reviewing this book.

Expressions of appreciation are also due to John Bennett, Executive Secretary-Manager of the San Francisco Commercial Club, San Francisco, California, for his assistance in drawing up the official rules for the Five-up game and to Ted Baker, Royal Robert Bush, Gerald F. Brush, Frank H. Case, Royce Chaney, Palmer C. Mendelson, Vasalie L. Peickii, August F. Riese, John L. Stanley, Frederic Teague, and J. E. Trabucco, who served on the advisory group and helped to formulate the official rules.

A special expression of gratitude is due to my friends Frederic Teague and Palmer C. Mendelson, who reviewed the book with skill and made many helpful suggestions.

I also thank the many hundreds of friends and domino players whose questions and suggestions told me what I needed to know to compile an original book on dominoes; to George J. Greenwood for many helpful ideas; to Dr. Robert Levit, formerly with International Business Machine Company, for checking the algebraic calculations on which the percentages and odds are based; to John L. Stanley for his careful review of the lessons; and to Harry M. Gardiser for his help with the name for the popular game.

DOMINIC C. ARMANINO

PREFACE

As far as I know there has never been published a complete book on the game of dominoes, even though it is known to have existed for more than three hundred years. This could easily be because of a more than reasonable amount of fear of an Explosion (the capital is mine) that would cause the sensations of the Magna Carta, the Declaration of Independence, to pale by comparison.

In my humble opinion Dominic Armanino risks life and limb as he volunteers to bring into black and white Rules of the Game, and, what could be most explosive of all, Suggestions on How to Play the Game.

But the man has done it, and the fact that you are reading these lines is proof positive that he shows bravery far and beyond the line of ordinary human duty and should rank among the Charlemagnes, the Marshal Neys, the George Washingtons, *et al.*

This is a domino book for thinkers, and, among opinionated people, no one is more opinionated than a domino player. As a matter of fact, your true domino-an is utterly convinced that no one plays the game as well as he does, no one could possibly have the utter grasp of its mysteries that he does, and, to cap the climax, every other domino player (and don't let this go any further) is a plain damn fool.

San Francisco is, if not the fountainhead of the popular Five-up domino game, certainly the headwaters. Throughout the club life of the Bay Area the game is practically the national pastime. Hundreds of tables at lunchtime attest to the devotion of domino players. Believe it or not, one of the largest and most venerable clubs in this city is building a separate floor to house nothing but a host of domino players, all of whom can and will debate fiercely (with swords, pistols, or dominoes) as to whether the 6-4 is a suitable set, whether you should play off your partner's spinner, and whether Mr. X will ever learn the game if he lives a thousand years.

They tell me the game is quite popular in southern California, Oregon, Washington, and also in a varied degree and form in Texas and other places throughout the United States, but you can bet your last tile that as the missionaries bring this inviting Five-up game to more tables of the Middle West and East, you will soon no longer hear the par-for-the-course observation of laymen on seeing their first domino game, "Why, I used to play that game as a kid."

Well, friends, as the saying goes, the San Francisco Five-up game "ain't for kids." It can be rough and tough. The four-handed version can give more pleasure, agony, aggravation, and sport than many a card game. And, of course, if you play for a bob or two, it could (possibly) add to the interest in the battle of the tiles.

But again to Dominic Armanino, whom I have intimately known through association in San Francisco's Commercial Club and San Mateo's Peninsula Golf and Country Club, congratulations on your book, your complete researching, your stick-to-it-iveness, all of which are worthy of high commendation, but most particularly, sir, on your pure, unadulterated bravery in venturing where most domino players would fear to tread.

PALMER C. MENDELSON

FOREWORD

While "Dominoes" has been considered by many to be a child's game, the Five-up version has become, particularly in the San Francisco Bay Area, sensationally popular in club and social life, and within the past ten years has practically become the basic game in virtually all the clubs in and around San Francisco. From this entree it has spread into the homes of the Bay Area until today it is estimated that more than one hundred thousand people are avid domino players in northern California alone.

Players traveling throughout the nation have developed interest in this great parlor game to such an extent that it would seem opportune to bring out a book, such as this one, detailing the rules of the game, the basic fundamentals, and suggestions on the play. Actually, there are many variations of dominoes, and many are carried in this volume. It is true, however, that the Five-up game is the most popular, and it is with this feature that we mostly concern ourselves here.

THE POPULAR FIVE-UP GAME

For sheer pleasure the Five-up domino game has no equal. It truly has all the qualities one would seek in any game, action, fun, relaxation. It is loaded with untold thousands of combinations offering opportunity to use a limitless amount of skill. It can never become boring, as each hand presents a new challenge.

Two, three, or four can play, and each player is an active participant throughout. The tide of winning or losing ebbs and flows and the game compels and retains the player's complete attention.

The popular Five-up game is for everybody—not just experts. It is easy to learn and anyone who can add, subtract, and divide can play the game and enjoy it equally as well as the next person. The fundamentals of the game are simple and can be learned quickly. The finer points can be acquired with a little study and practice. And with your improvement and experience the sheer enjoyment of the game will give you loads of fun. Thousands of homes have substituted dominoes for cards, and a set of dominoes and board are now standard equipment in fun rooms.

GAMES FOR YOUNG PEOPLE

Many parents have found dominoes perfect for teaching their children arithmetic, and it is amazing how quickly they learn. It encourages them to concentrate and use their minds.

The domino pieces represent numbers, and the games are based on arithmetic, the oldest of all arts and sciences. Certainly the use of figures is so important to all of us in our lives that our personal success depends to a great extent on our familiarity with numbers and our ability to use them.

There are several games for young children included in this book. These games are easy and can be taught very quickly.

IT'S A GREAT DISEASE

Expose yourself to the Five-up game. Get a foursome started and you will find that an evening with the dominoes can be one of the most pleasurable you could imagine. You, too, will find that you fancy your own system as the best and will doubtless have contempt for not only your opponents' game, but possibly (quite probably) your partner's. It is that kind of game. Novels could be written on the repartee of San Francisco domino tables, and you will find, after getting interested in the Five-up game, that you, your family, and your friends will actually revel in the pleasure dominoes will provide.

Give it a trial, you'll not regret it. Good luck—and good dominoes.

DOMINIC C. ARMANINO

CONTENTS

PART 1

The Popular Five-up Game

THE NEW TWENTIETH-CENTURY GAME

Five-up is an American game. It is the latest and most popular domino game played in the United States. It was developed into its present form in San Francisco in the early twentieth century.

The method of playing is very simple, yet the probabilities of this game are so great that each play presents a new situation and players never think of duplicate hands for guidance. They rely entirely upon their ability to analyze each play. The degree of skill that can be applied is limitless and can engage all of your talents. The luck and skill factors are happily so proportioned that defeat can always be attributed to luck and victory to skill.

The chances in the game can best be illustrated by comparison with a pair of dice. In both, the element is determined by the total possible combinations. In a pair of dice taken two at a time there are thirty-six possible combinations, but in a set of twenty-eight dominoes drawn five at a time there are 98,280 possible combinations.

The history of Five-up is one of gradual development rather than direct invention. The characteristics of this game are elaborations and refinements of the European matching games.

The original European game of dominoes has been traced back only to Italy, where it was played in the early eighteenth century. From there it spread through the continent of Europe and then to Great Britain. Etymologists do not agree regarding the origin of the name "domino." Some claim the pieces came to be called "domino" from their resemblance to the style of the facial half-mask çalled "domino."

Historical evidence as to the actual invention of dominoes is inconclusive. It has only been established that Chinese dominoes existed in their present form in China in the year A.D. 1120. They are clearly descended from dice, and particularly from a game with two dice which appears to have been introduced into China from India. The domino piece is a conjoined dice and the twenty-one individual domino pieces in the Chinese dominoes represent the possible throws with two dice. The Chinese games of dominoes are played with thirty-two dominoes, of which twenty-one are individual pieces and eleven are duplicates. These same twenty-one individual pieces are part of the European domino set, but the similarity ends there.

The European games are played with twenty-eight dominoes, of which twenty-one represent the possible throws with a pair of dice, plus seven additional pieces. Six of the seven pieces join one of the six numbers on the dice with a blank and the seventh is a double blank. There does not appear to be any connecting link between the Chinese game of dominoes and the European games. The peculiar Chinese games have philosophic-astronomic elements that are not present in the European games. The European games are purely arithmetical.

The Five-up game is the modern version of the European matching games. It has adopted the basic characteristics of the other matching games, enlarged the method of playing, and added scoring plays. All this has made Five-up an outstanding game of chance and skill.

THE DOMINOES

The set of dominoes is called the deck. The pieces are called dominoes; also bones, stones, and tiles. The standard set consists of twenty-eight pieces and begins at 6-6. Some sets start with 12-12 and some with 9-9. These sets are usually used for particular games such as Rum, which is played like poker with the 12-12 set, and block games which can be played with any domino set. The popular Five-up game and other domino games described in this book are played with the standard deck of twenty-eight dominoes.

DOMINO PIECES

The dominoes are oblong pieces, usually two inches by one inch, and approximately three-eighths inch thick. They are made of plastic or other materials. The face is divided into two sections. Each section has spots (pips) to represent numbers, or is a blank. One spot is used for each digit, thus five dots represent a value of 5, three dots a value of 3, and a blank the value of 0. The use of spots instead of Arabic numerals is what makes dominoes a game, as suits are matched and played instead of numbers. This makes the play automatic and simple to follow. The spots are hollowed out and painted a contrasting color, as black on white. The back and sides have no markings.

The twenty-eight dominoes have on their faces two numbers from 6 down through blank, i.e., 6's, 5's, 4's, 3's, 2's, 1's, and blanks taken two at a time. This is the 6-2:

THE SEVEN SUITS

All the dominoes with the same number belong to the same suit; the seven pieces with a 6 forming the 6 suit, those with a 2 the 2 suit, those with a blank the blank suit, and so on. These seven suits, numbers 6, 5, 4, 3, 2, 1, and blank, make up the domino deck, like the four suits of spades, hearts, diamonds, and clubs make up the deck of playing cards.

There are seven dominoes of each suit. These are the seven dominoes of the number 6 suit.

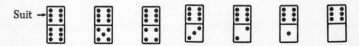

The seven dominoes of each suit have a number running from 6 down through blank. These seven numbers make up the suit like the thirteen cards from ace down through 2 in a deck of playing cards.

Do not be confused by the fact that in placing all of the dominoes side by side in numerical sequence there appear to be seven for one number and then, successively, one less for each other number. This is brought about by the fact that two numbers form one domino piece. This makes it impossible to set the dominoes up in seven rows of seven numbers. Each domino, *with two different numbers,* is a unit of two different suits. For example, the 6-5 is part of the number 6 suit and also of the number 5 suit.

Then, too, do not be confused by the fact that while each number appears eight times, there are only seven dominoes bearing the same number. This is occasioned by the fact that one of the numbers on the doubles is one of the seven dominoes of the suit and the other number is one of the seven numbers from 6 down through blank making up the suit numbers of the suit.

THE DECK

Seven doubles and twenty-one singles make up the deck of twenty-eight pieces.

One of the dominoes *of each suit* has the same number in both sections and is known as a *double*. There are seven of them, i.e., 6-6, 5-5, 4-4, 3-3, 2-2, 1-1, and 0-0. These are the seven doubles.

There are *six* dominoes *of each suit* having two different numbers from 6 down through blank. These are known as *singles* and there are twenty-one different pieces. These are the twenty-one singles.

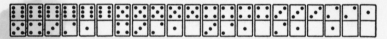

Turn all of the dominoes face up on the table and place all those with one particular number, say the number 6, side by side in numerical sequence by their suit numbers. You will observe that there are seven dominoes of that particular number. Study the other numbers and you will see that there are seven dominoes for each number from 6 down through blank. Notice also that each suit has seven suit numbers from 6 down through blank.

How to Play the Game

There are two basic fundamentals in playing the Five-up game —matching and scoring.

MATCHING

The game is played by matching dominoes. Each domino, as played, is laid face up on the table.

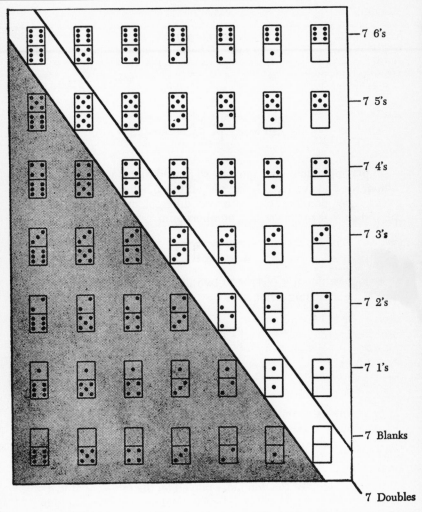

7 6's
7 5's
7 4's
7 3's
7 2's
7 1's
7 Blanks
7 Doubles

The twenty-one singles dominoes in the white section are also shown with their counterpart in shaded section. The domino deck has only one domino of each.

The first domino played is called the "set."

Each domino played after the set must match one of the open ends of the layout on the table. The number of a domino which is the extreme end of the layout on the table, or a double played on both sides, is an open end.

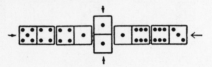

In playing a domino it must be so placed that it will match and adjoin the open end, a 5 being played to a 5, a 3 to a 3, and so on.

A singles domino (one with two different numbers) must be played so that two matching numbers join.

A doubles domino (one with two numbers alike) must be laid across the matching number.

SCORING

The game is a contest for points. The object is to outscore the opponents.

Scoring is done on the basis of one point for the count of five and each multiple of five. *5 = 1 point.*

Points are made in two ways. First, by making the total count of the open ends of the dominoes played on the table equal five or a multiple of five and, second, by the total count of the dominoes remaining in the opponents' hands after one of the players goes out by being the first to get rid of all his dominoes. The player who goes "out" scores the count in the opponents' hands.

The strategy is to score during play, go out, or reduce the count remaining in your hand and prevent the opponents from scoring.

GAME

The game is played through a series of hands until one team makes the necessary points to win. The team (or player) that reaches 61 points or more at the finish of any hand wins the game. If both teams reach 61 points or more, the team that is ahead wins. *61 points is game.*

A hand consists of a series of plays with the five dominoes originally drawn from the deck of twenty-eight dominoes. If a player is unable to play the dominoes in his hand, he is forced to draw from the boneyard (deck) until he has a domino that will play, and the dominoes drawn become part of his hand. The hand is completed when one of the players plays his last domino.

THE PLAY

The game is played by two, three, or four players with the standard set of twenty-eight dominoes. The four-handed game is played as doubles and the players pair off as partners. Each player draws five dominoes from the deck. The dominoes remaining are set aside and become the boneyard.

SHUFFLE AND SET

The game is started by placing all of the dominoes in the deck in the center of the table face down so that the spots do not show. The pieces are pushed around and shuffled thoroughly by any one of the players.

The players then draw to determine who shall "set." Each draws one domino and shows it to the other players. The player who draws the highest domino is "on set" and plays first. If the dominoes of the same value are drawn, then the one with the highest end sets, i.e., 6-4 is higher than 5-5. The method is the same in two-, three-, and four-handed games.

After the first hand the set rotates to the left (clockwise). It alternates in a two-handed game.

DRAWING HAND

After the set has been determined, all dominoes are returned to the deck face down. They are then shuffled thoroughly. In a two-handed game the dominoes are shuffled by the player who lost the set. In a three- and four-handed game they are shuffled by the player to the right of the player on set.

The player on set draws five dominoes first and then the other players draw five dominoes. In the three- and four-handed games the players draw in turn (clockwise), starting to the left of the player on set.

Each player places the five dominoes drawn on their sides facing him so that they cannot be seen by the other players. They may be arranged in any order he pleases.

BONEYARD

The dominoes remaining in the deck, after all the players have drawn their hands, are left face down and become the boneyard. They are set to one side for further use as provided by the rules of the game.

If a player has no domino which enables him to play to the combination on the table, then he must draw from the boneyard until he secures a domino that will play. In a three- or four-handed game all of the dominoes in the boneyard, with the exception of one, may be drawn. In a two-handed game, all of the dominoes in the boneyard, with the exception of two, may be drawn.

The dominoes in the boneyard are placed to the right of the player on set and remain there until the end of the hand. This indicates who was on set at the beginning of the hand and who will be on set in the next hand. If the dominoes are moved toward a player to facilitate drawing, it is the responsibility of the setter to return the remaining dominoes to his right.

PLAYING THE HAND

The first domino played is the "set," and any domino may be played. It may be a singles with two numbers or a double.

Singles   Double

The play rotates from left to right (clockwise). It alternates in a two-handed game. Each player plays in turn.

Any domino with a like number may then be played off of either end of the singles or off of the double.

Each number on a singles domino may be played on only once, and then the number on that domino is cut off.

6-4 cut off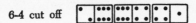

A double may be played on both sides and both ends before it is cut off.

5-5 cut off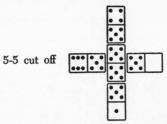

A double may be played on a like single number only, and it must cross the number. For example, the 4-4 played on the 4:

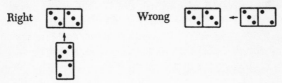

If the double has not previously been played on, the singles domino played off of the double must cross the double to form a "T." For example, the 3-2 played on the double 3.

When the double has been played on a single number or a single number has been played on the double, the next play on the double must cross the double to form a cross "+." For example, the 3-5 played on the 3-3.

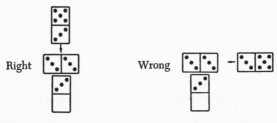

When the double has been played on both sides to form a cross "+" it becomes a spinner. Any singles with a like number may be played off of the spinner. For example, the 3-4 played off spinner 3-3.

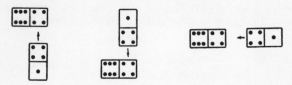

A domino may be played any place where it is playable. When a single is played on a single, it may be turned in any direction that will make it convenient to continue to play.

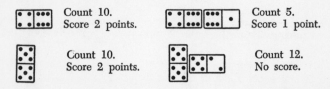

COUNT ON THE TABLE

A score is counted if the open ends of the dominoes played on the table add up to 5 or multiples of 5. One point is counted for each multiple of 5. If the count is 5, you count 1 point; if 10, 2 points; 15—3 points; 25—5 points, and so on. You try to play a domino which, added to or subtracted from the dominoes already played, will make a total of 5 or multiple of 5. If the count on the table is 13, you try to add 2 and make the count 15 for 3 points, or deduct 3 for a count of 10 or 2 points. When you play, if you are unable to make the count on the table 5 or multiples of 5, there is no score.

To determine the count on the table, only the open ends of singles dominoes and doubles which have not been played on both sides are counted. Here are a few illustrations:

Count 10.
Score 2 points.

Count 5.
Score 1 point.

Count 10.
Score 2 points.

Count 12.
No score.

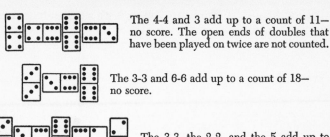

The 4-4 and 3 add up to a count of 11—no score. The open ends of doubles that have been played on twice are not counted.

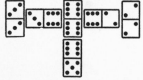

The 3-3 and 6-6 add up to a count of 18—no score.

The 3-3, the 2-2, and the 5 add up to a count of 15—score 3 points. The end of the domino played off of the end of the double is included in the count.

The strategy is to score by playing dominoes in a combination that will add up to a count that is divisible by 5 and, if possible, prevent the opponents from playing a combination that will produce a count divisible by 5. Preventing the opponents from taking a score is nearly as important as scoring.

COMPLETION OF HAND

The hand is at an end when one of the players gets rid of all of his dominoes. The player who plays his last domino calls "domino" or "out." The players turn their dominoes face up and the player who went out counts the spots in the opponents' hands.

CLOSED GAME

If each of the players has one or more dominoes, but is unable to play any one of them, the hand is "closed" or, as some say, "blocked."

If the game is blocked, all of the players turn their dominoes face up and count the spots on the dominoes remaining in their hands.

COUNT REMAINING IN HANDS

The strategy is to go out on the hand and receive the count remaining in the opponents' hands. If possible, the opponents are forced to draw from the boneyard, which increases the count left in their hands.

After each hand is played, the team that goes out receives 1 point for each 5 count or multiples of 5 remaining in their opponents' hands. If there are twenty-one spots, they receive 4 points.

What is left in the hand of the partner who goes out is disregarded. In counting the score for going out, the count of 1 or 2 above the multiple of 5 is dropped. When the extra count is 3 or 4, it is considered as a multiple of 5 and scored 1 point.

In the event none of the players are able to play and go out (the game is blocked), the team with the lowest count in their hands receives the count left in their opponents' hands for a score. In case of a tie count, there is no score.

GAME SCORE

The scores are recorded as they are made during the play and at the end of each hand.

The game is finished at the end of the hand during which a player or team makes the points needed to win the game. If both players or teams make game, the one that is ahead wins.

In case of a tie, two more hands must be played in the two- and four-handed games and three in the three-handed game.

KEEPING SCORE

The score may be kept on a "crib" board or by pencil and paper. The best way to keep score is to use a "crib" board and four round pegs. The standard board has two rows of thirty holes for each player or team. The holes are grouped and marked off in fives for easy scoring. After the first score is marked with one peg, a second is used to mark the second score. Thereafter the back peg is moved forward ahead of the front peg. In this way the score just taken can be verified by either player. Both players or teams should start on the same end (preferably the end nearest the center of the table), play down the outside, come back on the inside, and then continue around the outside until the finish of the game. This avoids confusion and shows just how each team stands at all times and all of the players can readily see the score for themselves.

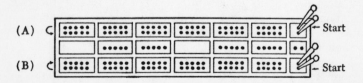

In two- and three-handed games each player pegs his own score. In a four-handed game each team pegs their team score and either player can be delegated to keep score. The scoreboard is placed between the two players who are keeping score.

Each player or team must take the score on making the play in order to receive credit for it. If score is kept with paper and pencil, it must be announced to the scorekeeper. Scores made but not claimed before the next play is completed are considered passed.

PLAY AND LEARN

There is nothing complicated about the game. All of the playing procedures have been explained in this section. The rules and finer points of the game will be explained later. Any difficulty you may encounter can easily be remedied with a little study and practice.

If you are just starting to play dominoes, place them all face up and make the plays illustrated in the following section on the two-handed game. This will give you good practice and a feel of the game. Second, get someone who wants to learn or has played dominoes before to play the game with you. In this way you will both get the benefit of practice and learn from each other. What one does not think of the other will. There is no substitute for practice and actual experience.

In the two-handed game you do not have a partner to worry about and there are not so many plays as in the four-handed game. So learn the two-handed game first. At first try to score. Do not worry too much about other possible plays. After you have played five or ten games you will find that you can play the game well and you will start discovering how to make more astute plays.

TWO-HANDED GAME—ILLUSTRATED

The two players draw five dominoes each. The eighteen dominoes that remain become the boneyard. The game is 61 points. Let's play the first hand of a two-handed game and get better acquainted with the basic playing procedure and rules.

FIRST HAND

We shuffle the dominoes and draw for set. You draw a 5-4 and your opponent draws a 6-2. You win the set. We return the two dominoes to the deck and your opponent mixes the dominoes thoroughly. You draw five dominoes first and then your opponent draws five dominoes. The remaining eighteen dominoes remain in the deck and are placed to your right. You turn your dominoes on their sides with the numbers facing you so they cannot be seen by your opponent. You drew:

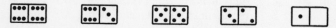

As you won the set, you play first. You try to make each move so you can follow your opponent with a play. You could set the 5-5 and score 2 points, but you are not sure that you can follow your opponent with a play. You decide to play the 6-6 because it will set up your hand and your opponent cannot score on it as you hold the only scoring domino, the 6-3. You play the 6-6. The count is 12. No score.

Your opponent drew the following dominoes and placed them on the table facing him:

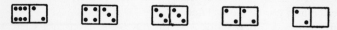

He looks over his dominoes and finds he has only one play, the 6-2. He plays the 6-2.

The count is 14. (Only the open ends are counted—the 6-6 and the 2.) No score.

You now hold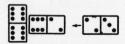

The 2-3 will play on the 2 and add 1 to the count. You play the 2-3.

The count is 15 (6-6 and 3). You score 3 points.

Your opponent holds

He looks at his dominoes and finds he has two plays, the 3-4 and the 3-3. If he plays the 3-4 you may have the 4-4 and score 4 points and he would be unable to play when it came his turn. The 3-3 gets rid of a double and gives you only one chance to score with the 6-4. He plays the 3-3.

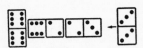

The count is 18. No score.

You hold

You look over your hand and find you have only one playable domino, the 6-3. It will play off of the 6-6 or the 3-3. If you play off of the 3-3, your opponent may have the 6-4 for a score of 2 points. If you play off of the 6-6 and he has the 6-1 or the 3-4, he can score 2 points, but if he should play the 6-1, it would put up a 1 which you need. You play the 6-3 off the 6-6.

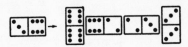

The count is 9. No score.

Your opponent holds

Your opponent plays the 3-4 on the single 3.

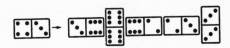

The count is 10 and he scores 2 points.

You hold

You have no playable domino and are forced to draw from the boneyard. You draw the 6-5 and play it on the 6-6.

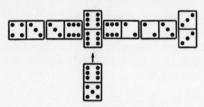

The count is 15 (4 + 6 + 5) and you score 3 points.

Your opponent holds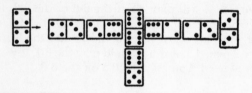

Your opponent looks over his hand and finds he cannot play. He is forced to draw from the boneyard. He draws the 1-1, which does not play. He draws another domino and gets the 4-4, which he plays off of the 4.

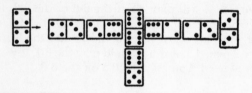

The count is 19. No score.

You hold

You play the 5-5 on the 5.

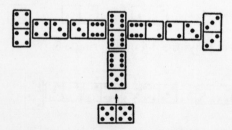

The count is 24. No score.

Your opponent holds

He is unable to play and must draw from the boneyard. He draws the 5-0, which he plays off of the 5-5.

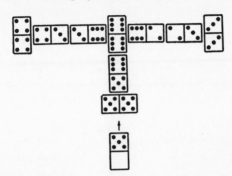

The count is 14. No score.
Your last domino is the 0-1. It plays off of the blank.

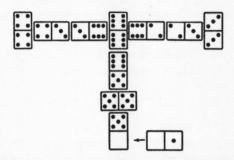

The count is 15 for a score of 3 points. You domino and go out. Your opponent turns the dominoes remaining in his hand face up on the table.

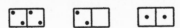

You count up the spots on all of the dominoes remaining in his hand. The count is 8. You receive 2 points. (One point is scored if the excess is 3 or 4, but if the excess is 1 or 2 it is disregarded.)

All the dominoes are turned face down on the table and you shuffle them thoroughly. It is now your opponent's turn to draw first and set. After both players have drawn, the dominoes remaining in the boneyard are placed to the right of the player on set. The set rotates after each hand and you continue the play until one player has scored 61 points or more. The last hand must be completed and the player who is ahead wins the game.

FOUR-HANDED GAME—ILLUSTRATED

In the four-handed domino game the players pair off and play as partners. The four players draw five dominoes each. The eight dominoes that remain become the boneyard. The game is 61 points. The basic method of playing and scoring is the same as in the two- and three-handed games. Generally the play in the four-handed game is more open than in the others and most players prefer the four-handed game.

Our purpose in this section is to explain and set forth the basic playing procedures in the four-handed game. The refinements, techniques, and strategy are explained later. Let's play the first hand of a four-handed game and get acquainted with the basic playing procedures.

FIRST HAND

The four players agree to draw and determine who shall be partners. They decide to rotate after each two games played. In this way each player will play with every other player as a partner.

The dominoes are all placed on the table face down. One of the players shuffles the dominoes and each player draws one and places it on the table face up. The two with the highest numbers are partners and the two lowest are partners. The player who draws the highest domino is on set. If the total of the two numbers is the same, the one with the highest number is considered the highest domino. One player draws 6-4, one 5-5, another 1-0, and the other 6-3. The players who drew 6-4 and 5-5 are partners and the ones who drew 6-3 and 1-0 are partners. The player who drew 6-4 is on set.

The dominoes are returned to the deck. North is on set. West "makes" the dominoes and places them in the center of the table. North draws five dominoes first, and then East, South, and West, each in turn, draw five. The remaining eight dominoes remain in the deck and they are placed to the right-hand side of North, who is on set. The deck remains there during the hand and in this way designates who is on original set and the player who will receive the set in the next hand. It is the responsibility of the player on set to have the dominoes in their proper place at all times.

North holds

He looks over his hand and resists the temptation to score. He decides to set the 6-6 instead. A good percentage play.

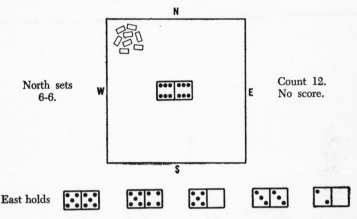

North sets 6-6.

Count 12.
No score.

East holds

He is unable to play and is forced to draw from the boneyard. He drew

and played the 6-5 on the 6-6.

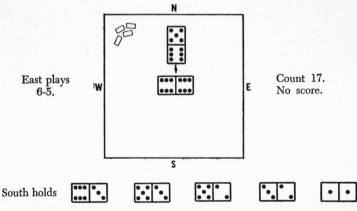

East plays 6-5.

Count 17.
No score.

South holds

He considers whether to play the 6-3 and assure his partner two numbers to play on or the 5-3 and score. As South holds the 6-3 and West cannot make all the ends 6's, but must put up a new number or the double 3, South decides to play the 5-3 and score 3 points.

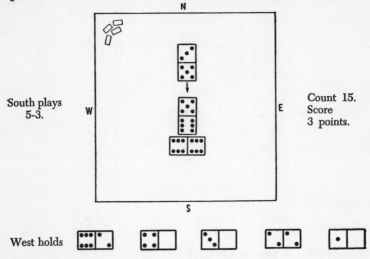

South plays 5-3.

Count 15. Score 3 points.

West holds

His partner went to the boneyard and cannot play off of the 6's. West decides to play the 6-2 off of the double 6, score 1 point, and give his partner one more number to play on.

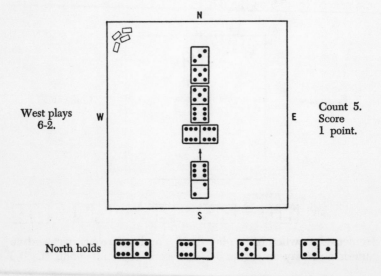

West plays 6-2.

Count 5. Score 1 point.

North holds

North has no choice but to play a 6 off of the spinner 6. He decides to hold the 6-1 and play the 6-4, which indicates to his partner that he cannot play on the 3 or 2 and he likes 4's.

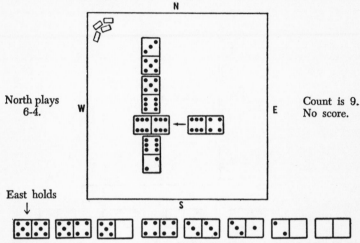

North plays 6-4.

Count is 9. No score.

East holds ↓

He has three 5's and two have been played. He can add a count of one and score so he plays the 4-5 on the 4.

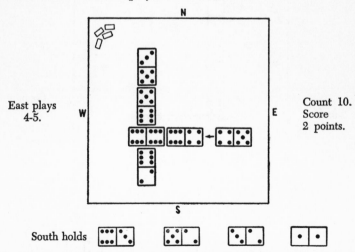

East plays 4-5.

Count 10. Score 2 points.

South holds

East has gone to the boneyard and South is on second set. South decides to play the 2-3 on the 2, to keep the 3's open in case his partner goes off set.

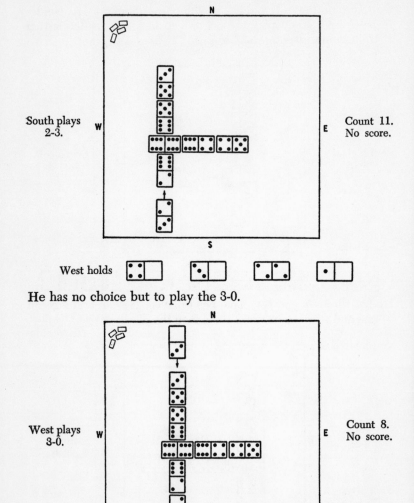

South plays
2-3.

Count 11.
No score.

He has no choice but to play the 3-0.

West plays
3-0.

Count 8.
No score.

North has three 1's in his hand and wants to assure going out. He
indicates to his partner he likes 1's by playing the 5-1 off of the 5.

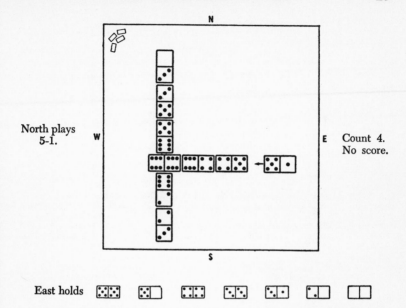

North plays 5-1.

Count 4.
No score.

East holds

East has a choice of playing the 5-0, 3-3, 3-1, 2-0, or 0-0. His partner put up the blank and his opponent put up the 1. He decides to play the 1-3 on the 1 and cut it off.

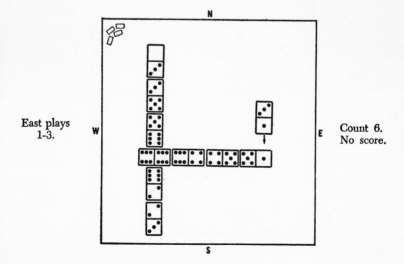

East plays 1-3.

Count 6.
No score.

South holds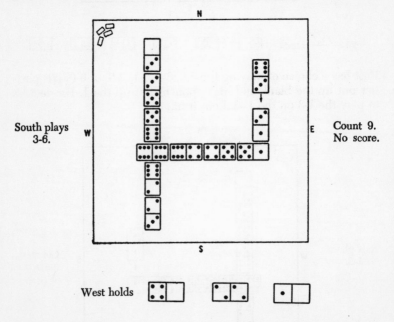

South attempts to play the 1-1, but it is not playable. He returns it
to his hand, but it must be turned face up on the table and
played at the first opportunity. South started to play the 6-3
on the 6 but suddenly realized his partner set the 6's and that this
play would cut off his partner's number. South changed his mind
and played the 6-3 on a 3, keeping both the 6's and 3's open. His
opponent, West, claimed that South's original play should stand.
However, all of the other players agreed South had not taken his
hand off of the 6-3 and his play on the 3 was allowed. A domino
is considered played when the player takes his hand off of the
domino. If he has not taken his hand off of the domino, the play
has not been completed and the player may change his mind and
play the domino elsewhere, but it may not be returned to his hand.

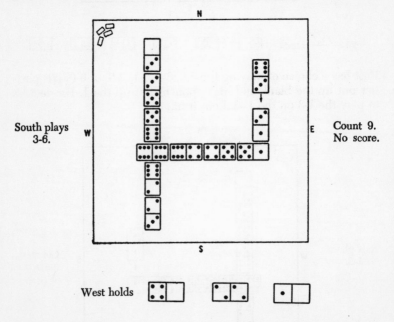

South plays
3-6.

Count 9.
No score.

West holds

He has the choice of playing the 0-4 or 0-1. He plays the 0-1 for
a score.

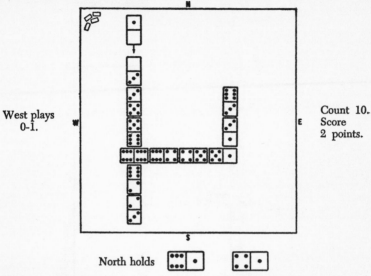

West plays
0-1.

Count 10.
Score
2 points.

North holds

He can play the 6-1 on the 1 for a score of 3 points or on the 6 for a score of 1 point, or the 4-1 on the 1. He does not dare take the 3 points because he would have no more 6's to play. If he plays the 4-1 on the 1, he cannot score, and he builds up the count. He decides to play it safe by playing the 6-1 off of the single 6. He scores 1 point and cannot be cut off, as he holds the 4-1 and only the 1-1 and 1-2 are out.

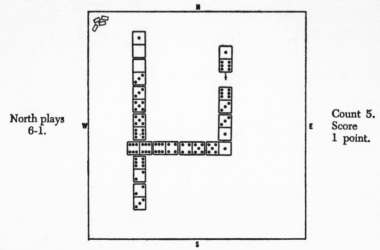

North plays
6-1.

Count 5.
Score
1 point.

East holds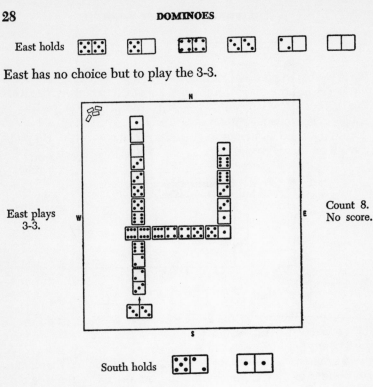

East has no choice but to play the 3-3.

East plays
3-3.

Count 8.
No score.

South holds

South has only one play, the 1-1.

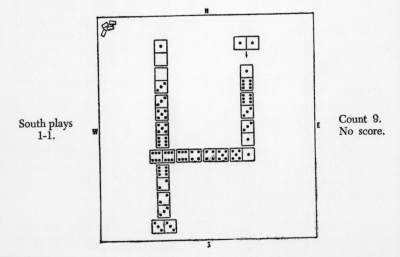

South plays
1-1.

Count 9.
No score.

West holds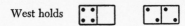

He is unable to play and is forced to the boneyard. He draws 6-0 but overlooks the play. He draws 4-2 and 2-1 and then discovers that he overdrew and announces it to the players. A penalty is applied. The opponents advance 3 points. West may not score during the hand and he must keep the dominoes drawn. He plays the 1-2 on the double 1.

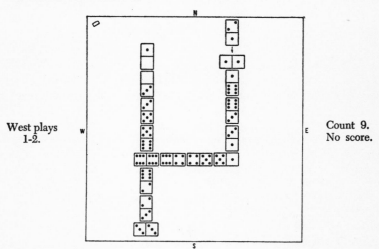

West plays 1-2.

Count 9. No score.

North holds the 4-1. He plays it on the 1 and goes out. No score. The count in South's hand (North's partner) is disregarded.

East and West turn the dominoes left in their hands face up. East holds 5-5, 5-0, 4-4, 2-0, 0-0. West holds 6-0, 4-2, 4-0, 2-2. North adds up the numbers and the count is 45. North and South receive 9 points.

A look at the scoreboard shows that North and South scored 16 points (4 on plays, 3 on opponents' penalty and 9 on the out) and East and West scored 5 points. This was a plus set for North.

The dominoes are all turned face down. The player who set the last hand mixes them thoroughly and the player to his left is now on set and draws first. Then the players to his left, each in turn, draw. The deck is placed to the right of the player on set, and he plays first. The set rotates after each hand, and the play is continued until one team has scored 61 points or more. The last hand must be completed and the team which is ahead wins the game.

The Players

Dominoes is a social game and it should be played so that it will provide the maximum of pleasure for all the players. This requires that the arrangements be fair and agreeable. It should be agreed to in advance of play who shall be partners, the rules of play, the scoring penalties, and the value of the points.

PARTNERS

In a four-handed game it is customary to pair off and play as partners. The players rotate after each game or the second game. In this way each player has an opportunity to play with all of the other players. Players are chosen by draw, and the two with the highest dominoes play together first. However, the partners may remain the same throughout if desired, as when one couple wishes to play another couple. Many couples who play together frequently put the winnings in a pot and then spend the money on an evening out together. This is a good way to get double enjoyment out of the game.

Sometimes it occurs that there are five or six persons who would like to play in a four-handed game. This is usually resolved by draw. The dominoes are placed face down and shuffled. Then each person draws a domino and the four with the highest dominoes play one or two games as agreed upon and the others kibitz. The two with the highest dominoes play the two with the next highest. After the one or two games have been played, one or two players go out to give the others a chance to play. The rotation is determined by the original draw.

RULES

It is a good plan to observe the official rules of play as set forth in a separate section of this book. This assures fair play and avoids embarrassment. Most of the controversies that arise concern overdrawing, misplays, and disclosed dominoes. Your special attention is directed to the rules on these matters.

Some players make the mistake of assuming the player on set has a sure out and disclose their dominoes before the last play is made. Frequently the player on set cannot go out and the other player has disclosed his hand to his opponents. Hold your dominoes and do not disclose your hand until one of the players has actually played and goes out.

ETIQUETTE

In playing dominoes you should be guided by good manners and courtesy of the table. For instance:

Dominoes should be drawn in your turn only.

When it comes your turn to "make" the dominoes, shuffle them thoroughly.

Every player has the privilege of shuffling the dominoes in the deck before he draws and the right to select any domino he wishes.

After each hand has been played, assist in turning dominoes face down.

When your opponent goes out, turn the dominoes left in your hand face up and let him count or check the score in your hand. Remember, it is his score.

Any player who asks is entitled to know how many dominoes are in your hand.

Joking, kidding, and needling are accepted as part of the game of dominoes. The horseplay and jest in advance of play are frequently like the friendly kidding that goes on in golf at the first tee. It makes for a lot of humor and fun. You should partake of the repartee that goes on, but keep it friendly. Let good judgment guide you.

ACCOUNTABILITY

It is your responsibility to know the situation at all times. If you overlook counts, scores, or misplays, it is your loss. Many players make it a practice to give their opponents a score that has been overlooked even though the rules do not require it. This should not lead you to expect such courtesies. Rather, you should be alert to all situations and each play. This means you should do these things for yourself:

1. Add up the count on the table.
2. Check your plays carefully for a score.
3. Verify the score claimed by other players.
4. Check the score pegged on the scoreboard.
5. Add up the count remaining in the opponent's hand.

It is surprising how often a score is overlooked or taken improperly, or a miscount is made of the dominoes on the table or remaining in the opponent's hand. If you do not verify the scores and counts, you will lose many points and games through careless and innocent errors.

GAME POINTS

The game is usually played for points and the team that wins the game receives the difference between the scores made by each team. If the winning team made 69 points and the losing team 58 points, the winner receives 11 points.

Many players like to play for points and game. The value of game is usually set at ten times the value of points. This makes it easy to keep the results of each player's score. If the amount agreed upon is one cent per point, the amount for winning the game should be 10 cents, 2 cents, and 20 cents, 5 cents, and 50 cents, etc.

RECORD OF COMPLETED GAMES

Any one of the players may be delegated to keep a record of the results of the games played. They should be recorded after each game is completed.

In two- and four-handed games where the partners remain the same, the player keeping the record enters the number of points his team has won and lost. In three-handed games each player's points are recorded individually.

In four-handed games, where the players rotate after one or two games, each player's points are recorded separately. The following method of recording the points won or lost by each player is recognized as the easiest and most accurate. A blank or ruled piece of paper is headed as follows:

John   Emma   Dick   Betty

If the players rotate after one game, the score is written after each game under each player's name preceded by a plus or minus sign. Subsequent scores are written under each name and the net plus or minus is shown for each player. The plus and minus figures should balance after each entry.

If the players rotate after two games, the scorekeeper writes down the points after the first game in the blank column to the right by showing his team as plus or minus. After the second game, the points won or lost by the scorekeeper and his partner are added or subtracted, as the case may be. The net or total plus or minus is then posted under each player's name.

By posting the points won or lost (which automatically includes any points for winning the game and double for skunks, if this has been agreed upon in advance), it is then simple to determine how much each player won or lost by multiplying the points by the value of each point.

PART 2

How to Improve Your Scoring Skill

YOUR HAND

The two basic principles, matching and scoring, have been explained and illustrated. Your next step is to learn the skill and strategy for making astute and skillful plays.

The situation where the player has a choice of plays occurs more frequently than the times where he has no choice. Where the player has no choice of play there is no skill involved, only the act of matching dominoes correctly. On the other hand, where the player has a choice of two or more plays, he has an opportunity to use his skill and that is what makes the game of dominoes interesting.

In the Five-up game of dominoes there are no uniform plays or patterns to follow. After each play the dominoes take a new form and a different situation is posed. The important thing is to concentrate on your present hand. The real skill is in the analysis of each situation—the ability to look at the dominoes that are in your hand and those that have been played—and then making the best play.

The dominoes drawn are the "tools" you have to work with. Your job is summarized in three words: visualize, organize, and utilize. Let's examine the hand so that you can see how to use the dominoes to your advantage.

THE ORIGINAL DRAW

Drawing your hand of five dominoes is like drawing a hand of five cards. One time you will get a hand which is long in one or two suits and short in others. Another time you will get a hand that is more evenly distributed. In some hands you will draw good scoring dominoes and in others you will have none. That is the luck of the draw.

While it is nice to draw a real good hand, you cannot expect to be lucky in every draw of your original hand. Most of the time you will draw an average hand.

AVERAGE HAND

What is an average hand? Based on the theory of probability, you can normally expect a hand as follows:

Suits (different numbers)	5 to 6
Suit length (matching numbers)	2 to 3 dominoes of same suit
Doubles	1 or 2, more likely 1
Lighthouse doubles	1 time out of 8
Singles (dominoes)	3 or 4, more likely 4
Repeaters	1 or 2, more likely 1
Kickers	1 or 2, more likely 1
6-1	One out of 5 or 6 hands
Average count	Total of 30

It is interesting to note that 50 per cent of the hand can be expected to be repeaters and kickers (including the 6-1), or two and three out of five dominoes. These are the sweethearts of dominoes. They are explained in "Score Repeaters and Kickers."

SUITS (DIFFERENT NUMBERS)

In dominoes void suits happen more frequently than in cards. In a deck of cards there are only four suits with fifty-two cards, whereas in dominoes there are seven suits on twenty-eight dominoes with fifty-six numbers.

The odds are 9 to 1 you will not hold dominoes of all seven suits. You can expect to draw all seven suits only one time out of ten; six suits 43 times out of 100; and five suits 39 times out of 100. Normally you can expect five to six suits.

SUIT LENGTH (MATCHING NUMBERS)

Three or more dominoes of one suit is a strong hand. You will have two dominoes of the same suit in practically every hand, no matching numbers one time out of 425, and you can expect to have three or more dominoes of one suit one time out of two.

THE DOUBLES

Each suit from 6 down through blank has a double, thus there are seven doubles. You can expect to draw one or more doubles 79 times out of 100 and two or more only 37 times out of 100.

The seven doubles make the game of dominoes both interesting and intriguing. If it were not for the doubles it would be a game of ticktacktoe. Many players fail to recognize the value of doubles in their hands and look upon them only as a disadvantage. Doubles in a player's hand may have more advantages than disadvantages, depending upon the position of the player and the circumstances.

The first and most important value of a double is that it provides four plays, while a singles provides only one play off of each end.

The second advantage of a double is that it can be played off of a single number to perpetuate that number and keep the game open.

 Four 2's have been played, and the 2 cannot be cut off.

Also a double played on a single number will set up a spinner on which scoring plays can be made with dominoes held in the player's hand. Then, too, doubles can be very useful to leave the numbers played unchanged so as not to give the next player a new number to play on and thus force him to the boneyard or force him to put up a new number. When a double is played, the chances are much greater of a new number coming up than when a singles is played, as a play-off of the double must be a different number.

The third value of doubles is that they can frequently be used to build up the count and add one of their number to the count for a score. The 5-5 and 0-0 are particularly good scoring dominoes, as the 5's and blanks are likely to come up when scoring starts.

The disadvantage of doubles is that they can be used only to add to the count and they are usually difficult to get rid of as there is only one way they can be played while there are two ways the singles can be played. Also, doubles can be made unplayable and become orphans. Thus it is important to know when to get rid of doubles and when to hold them.

THE SINGLES

Each suit has six singles. The seventh domino of each suit is a double. You can expect to draw five singles dominoes 21 out of 100 times, four 57 times out of 100, and three 72 times out of 100.

The 21 singles provide most of the action and change the picture each time one is played. Each singles can be used to add to or deduct from the count and they can be played off of a spinner.

One important advantage of singles is that each one can score six different ways while a double can score only one way.

The next advantage of singles is that they cannot be made unplayable. Only doubles can be made orphans.

The third advantage of singles is that if five singles of a particular number have been played and you hold the sixth single of that number, it can be used to make the double an orphan.

The fourth advantage of singles is that they serve as lead-back numbers. A lead-back number is one that leads back to the original number, and only a singles domino can serve as a lead-back number.

6-1 set 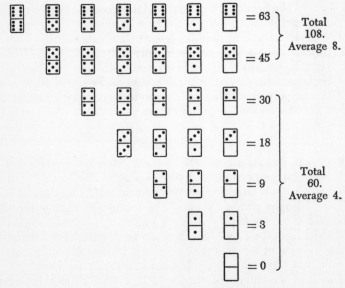 The 4-3 puts up the lead number 3 which leads back to 1 or 6 through the 3-1 or 3-6.

Other advantages of singles are that they can be used to block or cut off numbers, to tighten the game, to force new numbers, or to send your opponent to the boneyard. Then, too, they can be used to put up new numbers and open up the game.

AVERAGE COUNT

Observe carefully that the total count of the twenty-eight pieces is 168. You will also notice that thirteen dominoes, the 6's and 5's, have a total count of 108 with an average count of approximately 8, while the other fifteen dominoes, the 4's, 3's, 2's, 1's, and blanks, have a total count of only 60 with an average count of only 4.

Total of 28 dominoes = 168

The total count of 168 divided by the twenty-eight dominoes gives an average of 6 for each domino.

Based on the average count of 6 for each domino, each player could be expected to draw an average count of 30 in the original draw of five dominoes, regardless of the order of drawing.

After you look at your hand, the average count in both the other players' hands and remaining in the deck may be different if you draw a lot of large or small dominoes. If you draw all 6's and 5's it does not mean your opponent is holding 1's and 2's, but merely that the average count in his hand is less than 6 for each domino.

When a hand is being played the averages change. If most of the dominoes played are large, the chances are that the dominoes remaining in the deck or the other players' hands are small.

If all or most of the 5's and 6's have been played, the numbers remaining in the opponent's hand and in the deck will be small. In this case you should not expect to catch your opponent with a large count in his hand. Therefore, there would be little to gain in sending your opponent to the boneyard. On the other hand, if all or most of the small dominoes have been played, the players and the deck will be holding the large dominoes. With this knowledge you will plan your strategy accordingly. If your opponents are on set, you will dispose of the large dominoes, if possible, to cut down the count remaining in your hand.

ARRANGING YOUR HAND

When you draw your hand the first thing to do is to arrange your hand in the manner most convenient to you. This will help you get well acquainted with the dominoes you have to play with.

Some players arrange their dominoes by suits and some place them side by side with the highest numbers on the left and the smallest on the right.

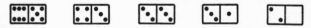

In this way you can run through your dominoes quickly and see if you have a playable domino and one that will play and add or deduct the difference to make a score.

When you have been forced to draw a large number of dominoes from the boneyard it is helpful to arrange the dominoes by suits. It is well to vary the position of the suits and avoid a set pattern that may disclose your strong suits to your opponents.

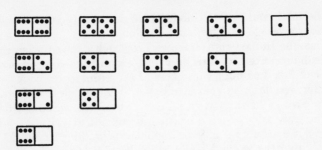

This enables you to count the dominoes of each number and locate the dominoes quickly and accurately.

CHECK YOUR HAND BEFORE YOU PLAY

Before you play, look at the numbers on the table and then the numbers in your hand and determine which dominoes will play. Next, check the dominoes that will play on open ends (singles, doubles, or spinners), and add or deduct the amount required for a score. For example, the 6-5 and 4-3 will reduce 1 or add 1. The 3-3 will add 3. The 3-1 and 2-0 will reduce or add 2.

It is surprising how often points are passed up or given away by a wrong or hasty play. To play skillfully is to think clearly.

SCORE REPEATERS AND KICKERS

The dominoes that will follow with an automatic score if the opponent scores are called the "repeaters" and "kickers." These are the blanks, the 5's, the 6-1, and the singles that will play off of their doubles and score.

Mathematically, scoring can be done one way with each double and six ways with each singles domino. Yet in actual play certain dominoes will score more often than others. This is so because the object of the play is to make the count 5 or multiples of 5, and plays are attracted to scores. Thus any domino that will play off of a spinner or another domino and automatically add 5, deduct 5, or leave the count unchanged after it is played, acts as a "kicker" or "repeater" and will follow with a score. All of these repeaters and kickers are singles with the exception of the 5-5 and 0-0.

The singles that will play off of their doubles and score are the 1-2, 2-4, 3-1, 3-6, 4-3, 5-0, and the 6-2. The 6-6, 6-4, 4-4, 4-1,

3-3, 3-2, 2-2, and 1-1 will not score if a score was made on the previous play.

When the scoring starts, it is very profitable to have the dominoes that can repeat or kick your opponent's score with your own score. The 6-1, 5-0, and 5-5 are the three best scoring dominoes in the deck.

REPEATERS (BLANKS)

All seven blanks are repeaters. The singles with a blank on one end will play off of their spinners and score the same as the previous play. The double blank will repeat on any blank.

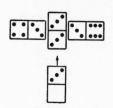

Played off of a blank—score the same.

Played off of spinner 1-1—score the same. (Also valuable to increase or reduce count by 1 to score.)

Played off of spinner 2-2—score the same. (Also valuable to increase or reduce count by 2 to score.)

Played off of spinner 3-3—score the same. (Also valuable to increase or reduce count by 3 to score.)

Played off of spinner 4-4—score the same. (Also valuable to increase or reduce count by 4 to score.)

Played off of spinner 5-5—score the same; played off of any blank—score 1 more; played off of 5-5—score 2 less.

Played off of spinner 6-6—score the same. (Also valuable to increase or reduce count by 6 to score.)

If your opponent goes out and any one of these dominoes remains in your hand, the count taken by your opponent will be small. It is good percentage strategy to hold these repeaters for possible play at the opportune time (with the exception of the 0-0, if you are on set).

KICKERS (FIVES)

Among domino players the 5's are called the "dancing girls." When scoring starts, it is usually very profitable to have these "kickers" in your hand.

Played off of spinner 5-5—score the same; played off of any blank—score 1 more; played off of 5-5—score 2 less; played off of any 5—score 1 less.

Played off of spinner—1-1—score 1 more. (Also valuable to increase or reduce count by 4 to score.)

Played off of spinner 2-2—score 1 more. (Also valuable to increase or reduce count by 3 to score.)

Played off of spinner 3-3—score 1 more. (Also valuable to increase or reduce count by 2 to score.)

Played off of spinner 4-4—score 1 more. (Also valuable to increase or reduce count by 1 to score.)

Played off of single 5—score 1 more.

Played off of spinner 6-6—score 1 more. (Also valuable to increase or reduce count by 1 to score.)

The 5-5 and all singles with a 5 on one end are kickers. The singles will play off of their spinners, add 5 to the count and score 1 more than the previous play.

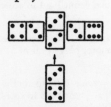

With the exception of the 5-0, these singles are of no value as kickers if their doubles are not spinners. As can be readily seen their count is much higher than the repeaters (blanks) if they are held in your hand when your opponents go out.

The 5-0 is a repeater as well as a kicker. It will play off of a spinner 5-5 and score, or play off of any blank, and score 1 more, or off of a 5-5 and score 2 less. The 5-0 is a real good domino to have in your hand.

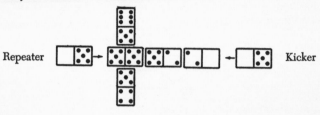

Repeater   Kicker

The 5-5 is a good kicker to hold because scores with 5's usually come up and it can be used to kick the opponent's score. It will play and score only on a 5, and when 5's are not started or played by the other players you may not be able to get rid of it; nevertheless, it usually pays to hold it and take a chance for a possible score.

THE 6-1

The 6-1 can be used to increase or reduce the count 5 and score 1 more or one less.

Played off of any scoring 1 it will score 1 more; played off of any scoring 6—score 1 less; also it is valuable to add 6 off of spinner 1 or to add 1 off of spinner 6.

It is the best scoring domino in the deck and a real good one to hold for scoring. Hold this domino for a big score.

DOUBLES WITH THEIR SCORING DOMINOES

When a double is played, the combined total of the double is included in the count on the table. For every double that scores there is a singles domino that will play off of the double and score. The scoring domino will make the same score, add 5 and score

1 more, reduce 5 and score 1 less, or reduce 10 and score 2 less.
There are seven singles that score off of the doubles.

Double played	Scoring singles		
0-0	0-5		Add 5 and score 1 more
1-1	1-2		Score the same
2-2	2-4		Score the same
3-3	3-1		Reduce 5 and score 1 less
3-3	3-6		Score the same
4-4	4-3		Reduce 5 and score 1 less
5-5	5-0		Reduce 10 and score 2 less
6-6	6-2		Reduce 10 and score 2 less

The 4-3 that plays off of the 4-4, and 6-2 that plays off of the 6-6
are easily overlooked. Study them closely. *The 3-3 has two scoring
dominoes,* the 3-1 and 3-6. The 5-0 scores on two doubles, the 0-0
and the 5-5.

THE SET

The word "set" is used to designate the first domino played at
the start of the hand.

The player who is "on set" and makes the lead play has a real
advantage over his opponents. He has the opportunity of (a) establishing the numbers in his hand to assure future plays; (b) of

taking a score; (c) of controlling his opponent's chances to play and score.

To make the most of his advantage, the player "on set" must set according to the dominoes in his hand. No particular domino is automatically a good or poor set. It is the matching dominoes of a suit that are important and the scoring plays that can follow on the set that make a particular domino the best choice.

MATCHING DOMINOES

In selecting the set, the first consideration is to determine your strongest suit. Ordinarily it is more important to establish your strongest suit(s) than to score.

As one or more numbers are missing in practically every hand, it can readily be seen that as the play progresses it becomes increasingly difficult to be able to continue playing. This is the time that the proper set pays off rather than the score taken when the set was made. You must resist the temptation to score unless the set is the proper one or a score is needed to avoid a possible "skunk" (a completed game in which the winning team or player scored 61 points or more and the losing team or player scored less than 31 points. An agreed penalty is usually applied).

When a double is set, four plays can be made on that domino before it is covered, whereas, when a singles domino with two different numbers is set, both numbers can be covered with only two plays. In a four-handed game a double assures the setter of at least one additional play, whereas a singles does not. If the setter holds a double, he can get rid of it only by playing it on one matching number, whereas a single can be played on two numbers. There are eighteen possible places a singles can be played, whereas there are only six possible places a double can be played. In addition, each singles domino will score in six ways, whereas a double will score in only one way. Thus, as between a singles and a double, it is better to hold the singles, as the odds of playing or scoring with the singles are much greater than playing or scoring with a double.

When a double is set, the next player's chances of holding a playable domino depends upon the number of dominoes left in the setter's hand with the same number as the set. If the setter held a double and one other domino with the same number, the next player has only 75 favorable chances out of 100 of holding a playable domino. This means that on an average the second player will be unable to play and will be forced to draw from the boneyard one time out of four. If the setter holds three of the same number before his set, the frequency the next player can expect to play is 65 out of 100, 54 out of 100 if the setter holds four numbers, 40 out of 100 if he holds five numbers, and 82 out of 100 if he holds only the double.

If a singles domino with two different numbers is set and the setter held five dominoes with a number the same as either number set, the frequency the next player can expect to play is 91 out of 100, 94 out of 100 if the setter held four, 96 out of 100 if he held three, 98 out of 100 if he held two, and 99 out of 100 if he held one.

A double is very definitely the best set when you hold one or more matching numbers. This gives you at least one or more plays in a four-handed game and at least two or more in a two-handed game. Then, too, there is a good chance that your opponent will be forced to the boneyard. Some players will not set a 6-6 unless they hold in their hand the only scoring domino, the 6-3. This is fallacious because there is only one domino that will score on the 6-6 and the chances of the opponent holding a particular domino such as the 6-3 is 18 to 5 or 3.6 to 1 against the opponent. The same is true of the other doubles except the 2-2, which can be scored on with the 2-6 and 2-1.

SETTING A DOUBLE

If you hold two or more doubles with matching numbers you should play the one with the longest suit or the one for which you hold dominoes that will play off of the double and score. The dominoes that will score off of the double will become kickers and come in very handy later when the big scoring starts.

Occasionally you will get a hand with two doubles and a singles that matches both dominoes.

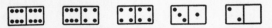

In the illustration it will be difficult to get rid of both doubles. Both the 6-6 and 4-4 will give the opponent a way to score. In a two-handed game the best play would be to play the 6-4 and score two points and then play one of the doubles when your turn comes around to play. In a four-handed game the 4-4 would be the preferred play to make. However, the position on the scoreboard may make it preferable to play the 6-4 and score two points and indicate to your partner that you like 4's and 6's.

The main problem for the player (or team) on set is if and

when the player should set a "lighthouse" double. Another problem is what domino should be set when the setter holds a hand with four or five dominoes of one number including the double of that number.

LIGHTHOUSE DOUBLE

A double with no matching number is called a "lighthouse."

Set

A "lighthouse set" is a double without another domino in the setter's hand that will play on the double.

One time out of ten you will draw a hand with only one double and no matching number. Now and then you will draw a sticky hand in which you hold several doubles with no matching numbers. Whether or not you would set a lighthouse depends upon whether the game is being played by two, three, or four players and the system followed by your team.

In a four-handed game the odds in a lighthouse set are in favor of the team on set, whether it is the 5-5 or any other double. However, there is a risk of the setter being forced off set in the first round of play when the setter's partner does not cross the lighthouse set. This risk is greater when a 5-5 lighthouse is set, as West will make all the numbers 5's for three points if possible, whereas he may not make all numbers the same in the case of other numbers. The alternative to setting a lighthouse is to set a singles domino which provides the setter with plays off of both ends.

Here is a guide on setting when you hold one or more lighthouse doubles and no doubles with matching numbers:

One lighthouse	Two-handed game	avoid
	Three-handed game	set
	Four-handed game	avoid—Exception: Set if partner follows practice of crossing (playing on) your set.
		See Part 7, Lesson 2.
Two or more lighthouses	Two-, three-, or four-handed	set

LONG SUITS WITH DOUBLES

Hands with long suits of four or five dominoes of one number happen infrequently. A suit of exactly *four* dominoes of one particular number, including the double, will be drawn one time out of 35. In one out of 117 hands the fifth domino will be a double. In one hand out of 234 the fifth domino will be a "lighthouse" double. A suit of exactly *five*, including the double, will be drawn one time out of 937.

A hand of exactly five of one number including the double is an excellent hand. Exactly four, including the double, is a very strong hand. Yet many players have a theory that it is better to set a singles when they hold five, and the odd or fifth domino when they hold four. They contend that the setter should set away from his hand. They claim his number will come up in the natural course of events.

An analysis of the setter's chances proves that the double of the long suit is definitely the best set with only two exceptions:

1. Two-handed game—five of a suit, including the double. Set one of the singles. This forces your opponent to give you numbers. If the double is set, you may be unable to play your fifth domino and be forced to the deck. By setting away from your double one of the other numbers in your hand is bound to come up and you are assured of being able to play and go out. When your number comes up, play your double at the first opportunity.

2. Four-handed game—four of a suit, including the double, and the fifth domino is a lighthouse double. Set the lighthouse double, provided *your partner* follows practice of crossing (playing on) your set if possible. See "Cross System," Part 7, Lesson 2. If your partner does not follow practice of crossing his partner's set, then the lighthouse set can be very dangerous and should not be played. When the lighthouse is set, the setter must, at the first opportunity, play his double or put up his long suit.

When the double of a long suit is set the *secret* lies in the setter's strategy after the first play. When five of a suit, including the double, are held, the setter must, at the first opportunity, put up another of his long suit to protect his hand. When four, including the double, are held, the setter must put up another of his long suit or play his fifth or odd domino.

SETTING A SINGLES

When you set a singles, select the one for which you have at least one matching number for each end. This is important in two-, three-, and four-handed games.

Set a scoring domino in preference to a nonscoring domino. Hold your 5's and 0's for scoring later unless you are loaded with 5's or 0's and want to set them up, or unless you do not have any other dominoes with matching numbers on both ends. The 6-1 and 5-0 are excellent scoring dominoes and should rarely be set.

Mathematically, some singles dominoes are very good sets while others are very poor ones because they give the opponent too many chances to score. In general, the 4-3 and 4-2 are very poor sets because they give the opponent four ways to score. The 6-3 and 6-2 give three ways to score. On the other hand, when the 3-2 is set, the opponent has no way to score.

SCORING SETS

In setting, the player on set should consider the points he can score and the chances given the second player to play and score. Let's examine each scoring domino and determine its individual advantage or disadvantage.

There are only five dominoes that will score when they are set: the 6-4, 5-5, 5-0, 4-1, and 3-2. Of these, the 3-2 is the only set that cannot be scored on.

Some players will set the 5-0 and score 1 point. Experienced players have rightly dubbed this play "idiot's delight." Usually the 5-0 is a poor set because it gives the second player too many chances to play and score. The opponent can follow with a score with two dominoes, the 5-5 and the 0-0. While the odds are 3 to 2 against the opponent holding either one of these two dominoes and scoring, these odds are more than twice as favorable for him than if another domino were played, say, the 3-3 where the odds would be 18 to 5 against him. Where a singles domino with two numbers is set, the opponent's chances of having a playable domino are about 96 out of 100, whereas if a double is set, his chances are only about 75 out of 100. In addition, the 5-0 is an excellent kicker to hold for play later.

The 5-5 is a good set if other matching dominoes are held. It scores two points and gives the opponent only about 75 out of 100 chances to play, and the odds against his holding the 5-0 for a score of two points are 18 to 5 against him.

SCORING

The object of the game is to score points and win. The two most important things in playing are scoring properly and minimizing your opponent's chances to score. More games are lost by overlooking scores, scoring less than possible, or giving the opponents unnecessary chances to score than for any other reasons. To pass up or give away points is a sure way to lose many a game. Scoring is a phase of your game that can be improved with a little study and practice.

Each domino has one or more scoring possibilities and can be played to add to or deduct from the count on the table or leave it unchanged. Study each domino carefully and you will soon see how each can be played for a score. In looking over each domino you will observe that each singles domino will play and score six ways, whereas each double will play and score only one way.

The most that you can add is 6, but you can deduct as much as 12 and score.

SCORING WITH DOUBLES

A double may be played only on a singles and will *score only by adding* one of its two numbers. Example:

Count of 7 raised to 10.

SCORING WITH SINGLES

Singles dominoes may be played on other dominoes, whether singles or doubles. Each singles domino can play and score off of other dominoes in *six ways*; three ways on each of its two numbers. Let's see the different ways the 6-5 can play and score.

1. On either double of the two numbers:

   (a) off of the 6-6—reducing the count.

Count of 17 reduced to 10.

(b) off of the 5-5—reducing the count.

 Count of 14 reduced to 10.

The plays off of the doubles seem to give most of the trouble. Playing off the double in effect eliminates it. The result, after the play is made, is the same as if the play was made on a single number.

Some singles, when played on their doubles, as the 1-3 on the 1-1, will increase the count; other singles will leave the count unchanged, as the 1-2 on the 1-1.

2. On either spinner (double previously played on) of the two numbers:

(a) off of the spinner 6-6—increasing the count.

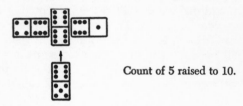

Count of 5 raised to 10.

(b) off of the spinner 5-5—increasing the count.

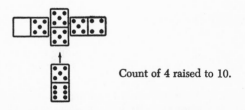

Count of 4 raised to 10.

Blanks played off of spinners leave count unchanged.

3. On either one of the two singles numbers:
   (a) off of the singles 6—reducing the count.

 Count of 11 reduced to 10.

   (b) off of the singles 5—increasing the count.

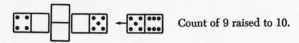 Count of 9 raised to 10.

LOOK BEFORE YOU LEAP

It is amazing how frequently players make a misplay and over-look a possible score or take a lesser one than possible. In this illustration the player had a 6-5 and played it off of the end 5 for 2 points instead of the 5-5 spinner for 3 points.

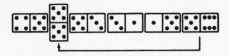

When the formation on the table becomes extended or the count is large and many possibilities are presented, it is very easy to overlook a score. Some combinations are confusing and must be looked over carefully. It is very frustrating when your partner has, say, a 6-1 which can play off of a 1 and score one more than your opponent by adding 5 to the count, and instead he played off of a 6, reducing the count by 5, thus passing up 2 valuable points.

Delay playing until you have looked over the situation carefully. First, try to add to the count for a score. If you cannot add to the count and score, then try for a play that will reduce the count and score.

DON'T GIVE YOUR OPPONENT UNNECESSARY
CHANCES TO SCORE

There is more to scoring than just taking points. A defense against a score by your opponent is one of the important parts of the game because it will help you decide when and how to score, when to pass up a score, and how to play to minimize your oppo-nent's chances of scoring.

The big trick in playing dominoes is to figure the play that can be made after you have played. If you can anticipate the next play, you can frequently prevent your opponent from scoring or playing or reduce his chances of doing either. Remember, your opponent probably has some kickers, too, such as the 5-5. If you score and he can play the 5-5 on a 5, he can score one more than you. If you can score and make it impossible for your opponent to score with his kickers, it is an excellent play. You score, prevent a score.

There are twenty-six ways to follow a score with another score and, of these, ten will increase the count and score. Only six ways will reduce the count and ten leave the count unchanged and score. If your opponent can follow with a score, the odds are 10 to 3 he will take the same or a higher score.

You can frequently avoid giving your opponent unnecessary chances to score or reduce the possible score he may take by doing three things.

1. Look over the dominoes carefully before you play and determine if the domino that would score or play, if you make the choice you have in mind, has already been played.

Example: It is your turn to play and you hold the 4-6 and play it off of the single 4, making the count 18.

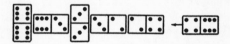

Your play makes it impossible for your opponent to score because the 6-3 and 3-2 have both been played. If you had played the 6-4 off of the 6-6, your opponent could score with the 6-2 or 4-1.

2. Do not be too anxious to get rid of a particular domino, such as the 6-6, and give your opponent too many ways to score or a chance to take a big score.

3. Determine the domino(es) that your opponent could hold and play for a score. Then make the play that gives him the least chance to score or play.

THE COUNT

Twice in two weeks an experienced player inadvertently passed up a score of 5 points on 6's. Once the player and his partner were skunked as a result of the oversight. The other time this player and his partner missed the opportunity to skunk the other team. An unusual coincidence? No. It is surprising how often a miscount is made or a valuable score is overlooked, particularly when large dominoes have been played or the count is high and there is considerable conversation going on to distract the player.

ADD UP COUNT ON TABLE

You must know the count on the table before you play. It is very helpful to keep track of the total count at all times, both before and after each play. This enables you to check quickly the correctness of your opponent's count if a score is taken and gives you a clue to the possible plays coming up. Also, it enables you to check your dominoes for the best possible play when your turn comes. Of equal importance, it enables you to play quickly and not hold up the game unnecessarily. Players don't mind a delay when an occasional difficult play is involved, as when you have drawn from the deck and want to check and count the dominoes played and those in your hand, but continual delay makes the game drag and it becomes boring.

You should always add up the count on the table yourself. Before you play, it is permissible for you to ask the other players for the count, but you are responsible for any miscount. Any plays you make based on a miscount must stand. Further, your partner is not permitted to suggest a possible play by either word or deed.

USE PLUS OR MINUS METHOD

The simplest, surest, and quickest way to find out how you can score when it comes your turn to play is to determine how much needs to be added or deducted from the count on the table. Then you look at your dominoes to see if you have a playable domino with the difference or number that is needed to score. Also, this plus or minus method is very helpful to determine how you can prevent your opponent from scoring or how to give him the least chance to score.

You may find the plus or minus method a little difficult at first, but after a little practice it will come to you easily and pay off handsomely.

It is a good practice to count from left to right, clockwise, starting at your left. This assures a quick and accurate count.

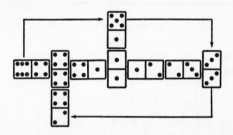

In the above illustration your opponent has played and you add up the count on the table. The 6 plus 5 is 11, plus 6 is 17, plus 2 is 19. With this total in mind you merely need to know how much to add or deduct to score. The total count is 19, so you know immediately that to score you need to add 6 for a count of 25, or add 1 for a count of 20, or deduct 4 for a count of 15. *This is the plus or minus system.*

Having determined the count on the table and what you need to add or deduct to score, you look over your dominoes carefully to see if you have one or more playable dominoes that will add or deduct the necessary difference to give you a score. In the illustration there are two numbers that will add 6 for a count of 25 and a score of 5 points, the 6-6 on the 6, the 1-6 on the spinner 1. The 5-6 will play off of the 5 and add 1 for a count of 20, or 4 points. The 6-2 will play off of the 6 and reduce 4 for a count of 15 and 3 points.

When you become proficient at keeping track of the count on the table and using the plus or minus system, you will automatically know the proper play without adding up all of the counting dominoes on the table and those in your hand. You merely add or deduct the difference needed to make the change you want.

For example: It is your turn to play. The count is 17 and you need to add 3 or deduct 2, 7, or 12 to score. The only scoring domino in your hand is the 6-0, so you play it off of the 6-6, deducting 12 for a count of 5.

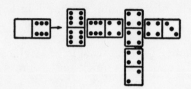

In keeping track of the count always reduce it down to the amount the count is over the highest multiple of 5. If the count is 21, you immediately know you need to add 4, or you may deduct 1, 6, or 11 to score.

ADOPT SIMPLIFIED COUNT

In adding up the count on the table many players omit the 5's because a small count is easier to work with. They determine the difference that needs to be added or deducted from the small count to make it a multiple of 5. The ends which are 5's score automatically.

Let's say it is your turn to play and you are going to take a count of the following dominoes that have been played.

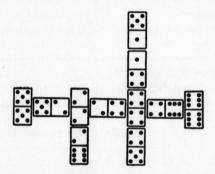

In adding up the count you can omit the four 5's and add up the three 6's for a count of 18. You need to add 2 to make the total 20 or reduce the count 3 to make it 15. You hold the 6-3 which you play off of the single 6 for a count of 15 or 3 points, to which you add the four 5's for a score of 7 points.

PART 3

How to Plan Your Strategy

FOUR BASIC PRINCIPLES

When you know the fundamentals of matching, counting, and scoring, the one important thing that remains for you to learn is over-all knowledge of how to make correct decisions in your choice of plays. That, in effect, means making organized use of what you know.

1. LOOK AT THE WHOLE PICTURE

You are constantly making decisions. You must decide whether to score or to pass up the points to keep yourself solvent; to give your partner a new number in lieu of taking a score; to cut off your partner and score or to pass up the score; to cut off an opponent's number and send him to the boneyard or to keep the game open. This is where a player can be a hero or a bum, smart or stupid, lucky or unlucky, and this makes for laughs and fun (and possibly murder).

The important thing is to learn the correct principles and then apply them to your game in making your choice of plays.

When a play has gone badly, a favorite remark is, "I should have played...." The opponents usually offer their deepest sympathy and frequently a crying towel.

Every combination of dominoes played presents a new situation, and rarely are any two alike. Usually there are two or more possibilities, and you must analyze the whole picture before making a choice. Whether the decision is simple or complex, it must be based on facts.

To make the right play, when there is a choice, you must consider who is on set, the position on the scoreboard, what numbers the other players were unable to play on, what numbers they played, the numbers they cut off, the score that may be taken, and how your opponent may be prevented from scoring. There is no single or general rule for the best play; instead, it is the situation that confronts you that indicates the right choice of play.

Make it your chief concern to "blend" your playing with what you have and your position in the game. If you are "on set," you must plan to "go out" on the hand. If your opponents are on set, you should endeavor to force them "off set." You must work in harmony with your partner and resist your opponents. You make the best of the dominoes in your hand and avoid wishful thinking. In short, your decisions are based on realities.

It frequently occurs that you will have several dominoes with a particular number, but you do not have the double to establish that number. Yet it would be helpful to your hand to have that double played. Under these circumstances your only hope is to have some other player, either your opponent or your partner, put up the double for you. To have your opponent put up the double, you must make a play that will give the opponent a chance or inducement to play the double. The best inducement is to give him an opportunity to score.

The way to bring out the double you want is to put up the number. If you want 1's, put up a 1. If you want a 6, put up a 6. This gives your opponent a chance to get rid of his double or your partner an opportunity to play the double. In addition, it is good practice to use the principle used by merchants of adding a premium to an article to induce buying. You offer the other player a premium by giving him a chance to score. You use bait to catch a fish and you use bait to get the double you want. So don't be afraid to pay the price, because this double you want will later become a spinner for you to play on and score.

If you have only one play, give the opponents the impression that you have a choice of plays. It is better to say, "There are two schools of thought," than, "Look at what I have to do."

2. SCORE

Five-up is a scoring game. You can't win and go out unless you score. Generally it is more important to score than to try to block an opponent.

Scoring in the right way and at the proper time is one of the finer points of the game. This skill can be developed with experience. When you can score, remember to add and score. However, there are situations where the position of the score or the dominoes played dictate a particular play that reduces the score such as preventing your opponent from scoring or going out or having a play. This is where your real skill can be displayed.

3. KEEP SOLVENT

A ship going to sea keeps moving ahead but looks out for obstacles in its path.

In dominoes, your opponent is constantly trying to block your play and send you to the boneyard. This can be very costly if your opponent is able to continue playing and causes you to draw many dominoes, thus assuring his going out and taking the count in your hand. To combat this situation, you must plan your defense as well as your offense.

One of your main objectives is to establish some particular suit and make it your prime number. If you hold several 4's, it is likely your opponent will be short of this number. Thus, if you have and play the 4-4, you are assured of your next play.

Frequently a player is confronted with the problem of taking a score and cutting off a number or of passing up points to keep himself or his partner solvent. To keep solvent and able to play is to avoid having to draw from the boneyard, and this means saving points.

4. SEND OPPONENT TO BONEYARD

Dominoes is a contest in which one player tries to overpower the opponent through skill and strategy. Frequently a properly executed offensive play can cut off the opponent's play and force him to draw from the boneyard. When this can be done it is quite an advantage and wins many points. Also, it is a great moral victory, which is part of the fun provided by the game.

However, forcing an opponent to draw from the deck can be disastrous to you. The opponent may get control of the game and a lot of dominoes skillfully played can mean a big score for your opponent. Ten to 20 points is not unusual. Careful thought must be given to the possible result before you make a play which you know will make the opponent draw.

In a four-handed game, forcing the setter off set automatically puts the player to his left on set. This is quite an advantage, since the side going out would probably have received 2 or more points. Instead, their opponents go out and receive 2 or more points for going out, making a difference of 4 or more points. As a general rule, your opponent to your left should be forced to draw if possible. It gets one of your opponents off of actual or possible set position. Some players make the mistake of trying to force the player to their right to draw. From this position it is practically impossible and usually puts the partner in trouble.

In a two-handed game, forcing an opponent to draw is much more dangerous and disastrous than in a four-handed partnership game. In the two-handed game an opponent should not intentionally be forced to draw unless: (1) you are sure of going out; or (2) you were forced to draw a lot of dominoes. In this latter circumstance you should try to reverse the situation and force the opponent to draw from the boneyard. Only in this way can you possibly turn a disadvantage into an advantage.

SCORING WITH KICKERS AND REPEATERS

Two or three times already this book has spoken of "kickers" and "repeaters" as if they were of equal importance with technical skill. For scoring they are more important than skill.

DON'T WASTE YOUR KICKERS AND REPEATERS

Kickers and repeaters should not be wasted, but held, as they will come in handy when the scoring starts. Too frequently a player plays a 5 and takes 1 point when it should be held for a 4- or 5-point score later. Sometimes a new number is given to an opponent in trouble for the sake of a score of 1, 2, or even 3 points.

When there is a choice, kickers and repeaters (5's, blanks, and 6-1) should not be played at the beginning of the hand. In most hands the high scoring does not start until the third or fourth time around. If you have played your scoring dominoes on the first or second time around, usually you have taken a small score and later, when the play comes around to you and your opponent has taken a large score, you are now unable to score, whereas, if you had held your kickers and repeaters you could play and take the same or a higher score. If they are held, you will score more often than not. This is not to say you must not score on the first or second round, but, rather, do not waste good scoring dominoes for a small score.

START 5'S WHEN YOU CAN FOLLOW

When you have 5's in your hand, say three or more, the odds are at least 4 to 1 in your favor that either one of your opponents does not hold two or more 5's. If your partner indicates he likes 5's, the odds in your favor are still greater.

When you have 5's and can follow with 5's you should put them up or start scoring with the 5's as soon as possible. This tells your partner you have more 5's and can probably follow with a score on any score made by your opponents.

SET UP YOUR REPEATERS AND KICKERS

When you have repeaters and kickers (blanks and 5's) in your hand and you have a choice of plays, you should set up your repeaters and kickers by crossing doubles with numbers corresponding with those on your kickers and repeaters. This will enable you to score when the play comes around to you. For instance, you hold the 3-5 and 3-0 and it is your turn to play. You cross the 3 and set up your 3-5 for a possible score later.

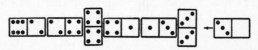

CUT OFF 5'S WHEN YOU CANNOT FOLLOW

The 5's are the "dancing girls" and the ones that score most frequently. If you do not hold 5's, then the odds are that your opponents have them. Naturally, they will do everything possible to start the scoring and keep it going. Under these circumstances you should not start scoring with 5's unless you can continue scoring with them. Instead, you should cut off 5's to prevent your opponent from playing 5's and scoring.

You can score with 5-3 but have no more 5's.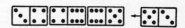

When you start scoring with 5's, your play indicates to your partner that you can continue scoring with 5's and that he should try to continue scoring. If you mislead your partner, it will cost you a lot of points.

WASTED REPEATERS AND KICKERS

If you are forced to waste a kicker, usually it is best that you play it off of the end of a singles rather than on a spinner. It reduces the count and the possible score that can be taken by the opponent.

BUILDING UP COUNT VS. REDUCING COUNT

There are situations where the count on the table should be built up and some where the count should be reduced. Frequently this move can mean the difference between winning or losing the game, or it might even result in a "skunk." It can mean scoring many points to offset a large count left in the hand or getting rid of a lot of large dominoes. The decision depends entirely on whether the odds are in your favor or against you. It concerns primarily the position of the players on the scoreboard, the number of dominoes in your team's hands, the number of dominoes in your opponents' hands, and whether or not you hold good kickers or repeaters (5's, blanks, or 6-1).

As a *general rule*, if you are unable to score, reduce the count. This reduces the opponent's opportunity to score and it cuts down any score made by him. A player follows this rule so rigidly that he is called "cut them down Bostwick." Generally this is a good defensive play, but there are exceptions that need to be made to take advantage of favorable situations.

If *you are far behind*, the only way you can catch up is to build the count and hope that your opponents will not score as much as you do, but you should not build up the count if, by doing so, you place yourself in jeopardy of a "skunk."

If your opponents are on set and your partner has gone to the boneyard for a lot of dominoes, your only chance of offsetting the count in your hand is by taking large scores. This can be done by building up the count and giving your partner a chance to score. A player with a lot of dominoes in his hand can frequently control the game, get rid of large dominoes, and make some very high scores. To cut down the count is to reduce your partner's opportunity of taking some high scores which would offset the count left in your two hands.

The position on the *scoreboard* should be watched carefully, particularly near the end of the game, or in the case of a possible "skunk." There are many times when the position of the score makes it advisable to build up the count on the table, and situations where the count should be reduced. The situation may exist during the play of a hand where you are in a position on the scoreboard of going out and your opponent is way behind. There is no reason to give him a chance to make large scores and possibly overcome you. Or the situation may be just the reverse and you are way behind. In such a case you may want to build up the count and try to overcome your opponent. The position of a score is like the score in contract bridge where one team is vulnerable and the other is not. Both bid what they need to make game. In dominoes you build up or cut down the count according to your position on the scoreboard.

HOW TO BUILD UP COUNT

When you are on set and want to build up a big count, set a small double. From an acorn an oak grows. From a small number big counts and scores develop. When the small dominoes are played first, the large ones must remain in the player's hands, and when these are played the count mushrooms.

A small set can build up to a count of 45 or more for a score of 9 points which can be repeated two or three times.

When the opponents are on set and you want to build up the count, play off of spinners and put up doubles rather than playing on a singles or crossing a double. Push your numbers and the one your partner has indicated by putting them up.

6-6 set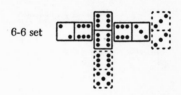

HOW TO REDUCE COUNT

When you are on set and want to keep the count low, set a large double. The bigger they are the harder they fall. From the large numbers you can only go down to the small ones, and when the large dominoes are played the players can only hold the small ones.

For example, you may be ahead 16 or 18 points and want to hold the scoring possibility down. You are on set and hold the 6-6 with a 6-3 and a 1-1 with a 1-5 with the choice of setting either double. Since you may want to hold the score down, you would set the 6-6 in preference to the 1-1, as the second player cannot score on the 6-6.

When the opponents are on set and you want to reduce the count, cross a double or play on a singles. Chop down the count.

Double blank set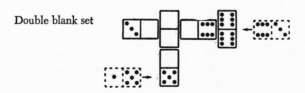

TIGHTENING VS. OPENING THE PLAY

The effect of one's play can be difficult to visualize. You may think your play is tightening up the game whereas it may actually be opening it up. You may believe you are hurting your opponent but actually be hurting your partner. Only by understanding your position in relation to the other players can you visualize the effect of your play. This is especially true when you are to the left of the player on set and two plays must follow yours before the player on set plays again.

The sequence chart below will help you visualize the position of the players, understand the effect of your plays, and follow the explanations and illustrations on tightening and opening up the game.

SEQUENCE CHART

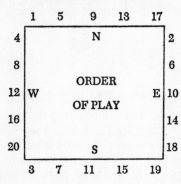

In a four-handed game each player draws and holds five dominoes and eight are in the boneyard.

North is "on set" and goes out on the seventeenth play unless he is forced off set.

GENERAL RULE

As a general rule, it is better to play an open game and score if possible. It is wise not to tighten the game unless it serves a good purpose and the odds in doing so are in your favor.

In a two- or three-handed game the problem of whether or not to tighten the game is relatively simple. You know what you have in your hand and you have no partner to consider. If you want to keep the game open, try to give yourself two or more plays so that your opponent cannot cut you off. As a general rule, do not tighten the game unless you have a sure out.

In a four-handed game try to keep your team solvent. The player who consistently tightens the game by cutting off the numbers that can be played on makes it difficult for his partner to play. For doing this consistently, a player in one of the large clubs has been dubbed "Cut Your Partner off George." His partners are frequently sent to the boneyard and after the hand is over he proudly announces, "I had nothing but 6's." So what?

When your partner is on set it is a mistake to try to send the player to your left to the boneyard. Instead, you must keep your partner solvent so that he may go out.

WHEN TO TIGHTEN THE GAME

There are three sound reasons for tightening the game. It may be done to force your opponent off set, to force him to put up a new number, or to control the game. Let's consider these three reasons.

Force Opponent Off Set

The *primary purpose* for tightening the game is to force your opponent to your left off set, thereby putting your partner "on set." Likewise, when you are "on set" you may tighten the game to force your opponent to your left off of "second set," thus putting your team on both "set" and "second set."

This means that there are only two players in the proper position to concentrate on sending their opponents to the boneyard. They are the player on set and the player to the right of the one on set. In the following example it is West's job to force North off set and put East on set if possible. It is North's place to force East off second set and put South on second set if possible.

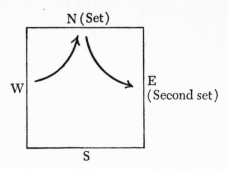

When you are in one of these two positions you should try to send only the player to your left to the boneyard. Concentrate on getting your man and your man is the player to your left. When you are not in this position, leave it up to your partner to try to send your opponent to his left to the boneyard, and avoid plays that will ruin his chances of sending the player to his left to the boneyard.

Many players make the mistake of trying to send the player to their right who is on set to the boneyard. They believe they can tighten the game for the player on set. This is a common fallacy. They do not realize that tightening the game from this position in effect opens up the play because it forces the opponent to his left, and then his partner, to put up new numbers.

When North is "on set," East's position is referred to as the "fourth position" from North's next play. Ordinarily East cannot force North off set from this position. Two plays must follow before North, the player on set, plays. East can help West, his partner, by not playing doubles on their opponents' numbers and not putting up new numbers and by cutting off opponents' numbers.

Frequently a player will set a singles and the other three players follow with plays with singles. Say the 6-4 was set. The second player played the 4-1, the third the 6-3, and the fourth the 3-1.

Here the original player's numbers were cut off and since the opponents played the 1's, the player on set could very well be forced to draw from the boneyard. This was an excellent play by the team off set, but the partner of the player on set made a very poor play if he could have played a double on the 6 or a singles on the first 1. If he held the 6-1 he should have played it on the 1, preserving the number set by his partner, thus:

Force Out New Number

The *second* reason for forcing an opponent to draw is to force the opponent to put up a new number that you or your partner need. A new number can frequently be forced by tightening the game and giving the opponent no choice.

Take a Big Score

A *third* reason for forcing your opponent to draw is where you can control the game and catch your opponents with a large count in their hands.

The time to really tighten the game is when you have control, because you hold all of the open or scoring dominoes. By controlling the game you can force your opponent off set and put your partner on set or assure your going out, or you have a chance to get rid of a lot of dominoes and make some nice scores. This is where it pays off to make a habit of watching the numbers your opponents were not able to play on and to count carefully each crucial number played.

HOW TO OPEN UP THE GAME

To open up the play, put up doubles, new numbers, or additional numbers. This gives your opponents more chances to play and score, but it helps keep your team solvent. This is very important when you or your partner are on set and your opponents were forced to draw a lot of dominoes from the boneyard.

The chances of your having all seven numbers when you draw your original hand is only 1 out of 10. As you and your partner play, you will have less and less numbers to play. The more doubles played and single numbers open, the better your chances of playing. If your partner has indicated he likes a number, play a double on it or play that number off of another double, if possible.

HOW TO TIGHTEN THE GAME

To tighten the game and make it more difficult for the opponent to play, reduce the open numbers. This gives your opponent less numbers to play on, reduces his chances to play, and gives him less opportunity to score.

Avoid putting up doubles, as this perpetuates the number and gives the opponent to your left an opportunity to play a new number on it. Play on a singles number and cut off the numbers put up by the opponents.

CLOSING THE GAME

When there are no playable dominoes in any of the players' hands or in the boneyard, the game is closed. The player whose turn it is to play must draw all of the dominoes in the boneyard except the last one in both the four- and three-handed games and the last two in a two-handed game.

The opportunity of closing the game so that no player can make another play occurs infrequently, but when it does, the player who is in a position to do so must make sure his move is right and rewarding. Otherwise he may be caught with a big count which may prove very costly. It is surprising how many times players overlook a domino or miscount a particular number and fall into a costly play.

There are two things to determine before you close the game: which team is most likely to have the largest count and would it be better to count a big score and keep the game open.

Calculated risk: Since the average count of each domino is 6, a fair guide is to count the number of dominoes in your opponents' hands and the dominoes in the boneyard which they will be forced to draw and then multiply the number of dominoes by 6 for their possible count. If most of the dominoes played are large numbers such as the 6-6, then the average will be less than 6. Add up the count in your hand and compare this to your estimate of the count in your opponents' hands. This is very important, as the count frequently means a difference of 5 or more points.

Scoring: If you have an opportunity to take a score that cannot be followed up with a play by your opponents because you control all of the playable dominoes, you should keep the play open. If you can take a score that is larger than the possible count in the opponents' hand, by all means take the score.

The Finish

Of all the things you have learned about playing dominoes (and this includes all of the major points we have taken up) you need to be more conscious of one thing than anything else. You've got to make 61 points or more first.

Although it is correct to say that every play is important to each game, it is a fact that frequently the prize is waiting for the team who does the best job toward the end of the game. It is during this latter part of the game that you must consider the position of each team on the scoreboard. On the basis of your position you plan your strategy and then play according to your strategy. If your position on the scoreboard is way behind that of your opponents, you will go all out to score, first, to prevent a "skunk" and, secondly, to overtake your opponents. On the other hand, if you are way ahead, you will play it "safe" and prevent your opponents from taking big scores, if possible. Your strategy is to maintain your lead.

It is the competitive spirit of the players that makes any game of sport interesting. This is true of dominoes. However, the game of dominoes differs from games in which each player's strategy is strictly offensive. Dominoes is a contest in which the strategy is both offensive and defensive. In the closing period of the game you must adopt the strategy that gives you the best chance to win.

The whole art of playing dominoes is to win. The way to win is to do every sportsmanlike thing possible to make 61 points or more first.

PART 4

How to Evaluate Specific Plays

Information Gained from Play

The president of a large bank was playing a game of dominoes with a friend. As the game proceeded down to the last play of the hand the president of the bank said to his friend, "You have the 2-2 in your hand," and then cut off the only 2 open on the table. The 2-2 was the domino in the player's hand and he was forced to the boneyard for a load. The friend asked in amazement, "How could you tell I held the 2-2?" "Ah," replied the banker, "that is a secret I learned from the Monks in Tibet."

The feat of the banker was not psychic or a trick of any kind. Strange as it may seem, the secret is *not a secret*. Anyone can do it. What the banker really did was to observe what numbers his opponent could not play on.

Every play conveys some significant information. The knowledge gained during the play of the hand can be very helpful. It is one of your most helpful aids in making a choice of plays. It may enable you to score with impunity, force your opponent to the boneyard, enable you to control the game, or indicate help is needed by your partner. Important facts and conclusions can be drawn from each play if you observe who made the play and when it was made. Yet many players promptly forget which player made a particular play as if it were trivial.

DIRECT AND INDIRECT INFORMATION

A good deal of the information afforded during the play of the hand is self-evident, such as the player on set; the domino set; your opponent's plays; your partner's plays; how many dominoes of a suit have been played, etc. All of this is direct information. Then there is the knowledge that can be gained from indirect information. It is information that can be concluded logically by inference.

The fact that a certain domino was played can prove that another different play could not be made. In another play a particular number that is put up may indicate the player wants that number left open. In each instance the conclusion is reached by inference logically deduced from the play made. Knowledge gained in this way is reliable and valuable. Such information is acted upon regularly and is the basis of sound plays.

The inference resulting from a play made by your partner or your opponent depends upon two factors, the circumstances at the time of the play, and whether the play was made voluntarily or involuntarily. Thus the indirect information that is derived from a play can be affirmative or negative, compulsive or neutral.

By carefully observing the dominoes that are played by your partner and your opponents and the way in which they are played you can get a clue to the numbers they hold or are missing in their hands. With this information you can put up the numbers that suit you and help your partner, or you can cut off those numbers that you do not want open.

AFFIRMATIVE PLAYS

A player's long suit gives him the best odds of all his plays, and most players make it a practice to lead from strength. The position of a player to the "set" and the circumstances surrounding his play may indicate that the player likes a particular number or prefers to follow a certain strategy.

Player on set: The player on set will usually set a double that provides another play or a singles that provides a play-off of each end. The numbers set must be considered his suits.

For example, your partner is on set and played the 4-5. It is your turn to play and you can turn both ends into 4's. There is no reason to assume he set away from his hand, and the only logical conclusion that can be drawn is that he has both 4's and 5's. So you trust your partner and make both ends 4's, hoping to send your opponent to your left to the boneyard.

Player on second set: This player will usually put up the number of his longest suit if he plays without taking a score. However, if he scores or makes a play to prevent a score, his play may not be an indicator and the number played off of the set may or may not be his strong suit.

Indicator: The size of the number, such as a 6 or 1, does not indicate that the player wants large or small numbers. It is the particular number that is indicated, not large or small. If your partner pushes 6's, he wants 6's, not 5's.

Score started with 5's: When a player can score and follow with 5's it can be very profitable to start the 5's. A player who starts scoring with 5's is indicating he can follow with 5's.

For example: North set the 4-4, East played the 4-2, South played the 4-5, and West played a 2-5, making both ends 5's.

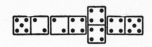

Since South put up the original 5, West's play indicates he has 5's or he would not have set them up. His play is literally shouting he has 5's and probably the 5-5.

Player pushing a number: A player who is endeavoring to send his opponent to the boneyard, or attempting to gain control, will push his long suit. This is particularly true when the player was sent to the boneyard.

For example: North set the 5-5. East went to the boneyard for a load and drew down to the last domino before he could play. He drew and played the 5-1. On the second time around East played the 4-6 on the 4.

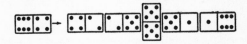

East's play indicates he likes 6's and probably has control of 6's. When it comes West's turn to play he must play off of the 5-5 if possible. If not, he should put up the 6-6 if he has it, which will probably force North to play off of his 5-5 and give East a chance to turn it into a 6. Very often this situation can be turned into a bonanza by East and West. As East has most of the dominoes, West must accept the information given by East's plays and try to get control to score heavily, or to send the opponents to the boneyard, or both.

Building up count: "Cut them down if you can't score" is a maxim generally followed to reduce the opponents' opportunity to score. If a player builds up the count you can be reasonably sure he holds good scoring dominoes or he has some other good reason for building the count.

Player forced to draw: The player who is forced to draw is in trouble. Your opponent's bad luck is your good luck because you have definite proof of the numbers missing in his hand. When there are several numbers that your opponent cannot play on, frequently he will have a double of a different number.

For example: Your opponent in a two-handed game set the 3-3. On the fourth play you played the 2-0 on the 2. Your opponent was unable to play and was forced to draw. He drew the 6-5 and played it on the spinner 6. You were unable to play, went to the boneyard, and drew the 3-1. Your opponent is still unable to play and is forced to draw. You now know he holds the 2-2 because it is the only number missing.

NEGATIVE PLAYS

When a player has a poor hand and is short of kickers and repeaters, he will reduce the count and get the hand over with as quickly and cheaply as possible. This can be detected mainly by the way his plays are made.

Player cuts 5's: When a player is short of 5's he does not want 5's started. This would give his opponents an opportunity to take big scores. When he cuts off a 5, it is apparent he is short of 5's.

For example: North set the 4-4, East played the 4-2, South played the 4-5, and West played the 5-2, making both ends 2's.

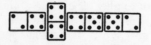

By passing up a score of two points, West's play indicates he does not have 5's and does not want them set up. Also, he is indicating he has a poor hand and wants the count reduced.

Player cuts number: When a player cuts off numbers, particularly without taking a score, he is indicating he does not like that number open or that he wants the count reduced.

Player reduces count: A player ordinarily will not play off of a double without scoring and set it up as a spinner for his opponents unless he wants the count reduced. A play-off of a double without scoring would tend to indicate that the player wants the count reduced and the scoring kept low.

COMPULSIVE PLAYS

A player would not waste a valuable kicker or repeater or give his opponent an opportunity to take a large score unless he was compelled to make that particular play. Forced plays are fairly easy to diagnose and the information gained is very reliable.

Wasted kickers and repeaters: When a player plays a good kicker or repeater without scoring, that player is "bleeding" because he would not waste a kicker if he had another play.

In the following illustration North set the 4-4 and East played the 4-5.

The 4-5 was probably a forced play, as South would not voluntarily waste this valuable kicker or East is loaded with 5's and is signaling his partner to play 5's at every opportunity. When it comes West's turn to play he should play off of the 4-4 if he can and give his partner a number to play on because North will figure East has no 4's and will try to send him to the boneyard. If East is loaded with 5's, each play-off of the 4 is a lead-back number to his 5's.

Plays off of a double: A player will usually hold a domino that plays off of a double because he is assured of another play.

For example: North, your partner, set the 1-1 and now he has played the 3-5 on the 3-3.

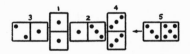

Your partner has no 2's and may be in trouble. He would not have played the 3-5 off the 3-3, wasting a good kicker, if he could have played on South's 2. When your turn comes, you should play off the 2 and give him a new number, or play a double on either his 5 or any new number that is put up.

Wasted scoring singles on doubles: A player would not waste a singles that will score off its double, but hold it for possible scoring later.

Example: It is East's turn, and he played the 1-2 on the 1-1.

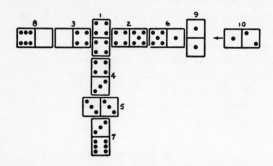

The player cannot play on the 6, because he would not play a 2 off of the 1-1, wasting a sure play and giving his opponent a new number to play on and score. If he had a 6, he would have played it and held his 1-2 which is a scoring domino off the 1-1.

Wasted plays on spinners: When a player plays off of a spinner without scoring, it is an indication that that player cannot play on any singles that are open. Usually the player is in trouble or, as some say, "bleeding," because he has to waste a valuable domino that could be very useful later.

Example: The 4-4 was set and East played on the spinner 4.

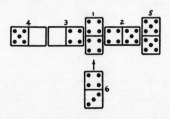

East cannot play on the 5's or he would not have played on the spinner 4, building up the count and giving South an opportunity to score 3 or 4 points. If he had a 5, he certainly would have played off of the 5-5, cutting the count down.

Example: The setter wants to preserve his set position and his plays usually are the easiest to diagnose. In the following illustration the player on set played a kicker off of his set without scoring.

North set the 6-6 and now plays the 6-5.
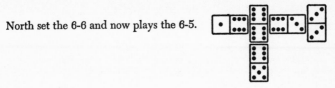

North is probably in trouble (or has 5's) because he would not have wasted the 6-5 on his set. He has no 1's or 3's and is out of 6's. His partner must give him a new number, if possible, because West will try to force North off set.

NEUTRAL PLAYS

A play can mean a lot or it can mean nothing at all. A great many plays do not convey any definite information. Whether or not they have any significance cannot be determined. Under these circumstances the best thing to do is to play an open game and score, if possible.

Suppose, for example, that your partner set the 2-2 and it is now his turn to play. He plays the 2-1 off of his original set.

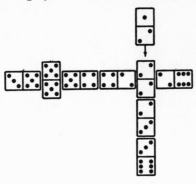

It is very obvious he cannot follow with the 2-5 and probably he cannot play on the 6 or 3, or he may have the 1-0 or 1-5 or he may be getting rid of a bad domino before someone else cuts off the 2. When your turn comes to play, you should give him a new number. You would not cut off the 1. You count the 6's and 5's and see that three 5's have been played and only two 6's, so you go off the 5's. He did not set 5's and, furthermore, his 1 is a lead back to the 1-5 if the 5's should be cut off.

PART 5

How to Master Suit Control

Suits

Domino players usually refer to the dominoes of one number merely by identifying the number, as 6's, 5's, or 3's. A player will say, "Six 5's have been played and the 5-3 is out." Rarely will you hear a player refer to the dominoes of one number as a suit. However, all of the dominoes of one number actually belong to the same suit, and they are designated here as a suit in order to identify the dominoes and to demonstrate the manner in which they may be played or controlled. Without this system of classifying the numbers it would be very confusing to the reader. So, regardless of which term is used, be it suits or numbers, the principle is the same.

Each of the two numbers on the twenty-eight dominoes serves two different functions. Each number serves both as a suit and as a suit number. It is this dual capacity of each number that gives the game its elusive characteristics. It is this two-way combination that makes it hard for many players to understand how to control the seven dominoes of each suit.

A member of a large club who has played dominoes over a period of twenty-five years was playing with friends and lost six straight games. Being completely frustrated by his plight, he remarked to his friends, "I just don't understand this game—someday I am going to learn what it's all about." The trouble with this player was that after twenty-five years of playing he knew little about suit control, the top level skill in playing dominoes. Any wonder he doesn't know what it's all about?

The way you play the dominoes of each suit can open up the game and give additional plays or it can tighten the game and force a player to the boneyard. You can block numbers or establish them. You can put up a number that will lead back to a player's number or prevent it. Your play can make a double unplayable or secure a play with it. It is all in the way you handle the seven dominoes of each suit.

You can sharpen up your playing skill by learning how to handle the seven dominoes of each suit. This will enable you to use or prevent the playback, one of the smartest plays in dominoes. With this skill you will know how to make the seven dominoes of each suit work for you and against your opponents.

THE SIX LEAD-BACK NUMBERS

Each of the seven suits has seven suit numbers from 6 down through blank. Six of the suit numbers are lead-back numbers. They are the numbers on the six singles.

Suit

Suit numbers →

Each single can be played on any domino that *puts up* one of the suit numbers. The play is called a playback. The number on the playback domino that matches a suit number is called a lead-back number. It produces a play with the matching domino of the particular suit. Let's take the 6-4 of the 6 suit.

Suit . . . .

Suit number . . . .

(Playback) . . . .

Lead-back number . .

Suit number . . . .

Original suit . . . .

The double has no lead-back number. This is so because the suit and suit number of the double are one and the same. The double can be played only on its own suit. Consequently, the suit number of the double is automatically eliminated as a lead-back number.

As each singles domino of the suit is played, that suit number is eliminated as a lead-back number.

For example, the 6-4 and 6-1 are played out of the 6 suit:

Suit

Suit numbers

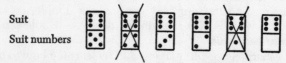

The 4 and 1 are no longer lead-back numbers for the 6 suit. The suit numbers 5, 3, 2, and blank remain as lead-back numbers.

As additional dominoes of the suit are played the lead-back numbers are reduced.

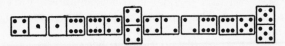

In the above illustration the 3 and blank remain as the only lead-back numbers for the 6 suit.

DOUBLE PLAYED

When a double has been played, a lead-back number to that suit cannot be given by playing on the double. As each domino of that suit is played, the suit number on that particular domino is eliminated as a lead-back number.

For example, the 6-6 is set and 6-4 is played.

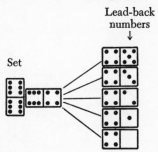

In the above illustration the suit number 4 has been played. There are five lead-back numbers left, the 5, 3, 2, 1, and blank.

SINGLES PLAYED

A singles has two suits, and when it is played both numbers are eliminated as suit numbers. For example, the 6-0 is set:

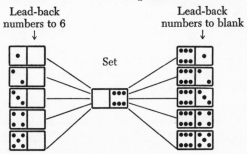

In the above illustration the blank is no longer a lead-back number for the 6, and the 6 is no longer a lead-back for the blank. While there were six original lead-back numbers for each suit, there are now five. The five lead-back numbers remaining for the blank and for the 6 are the 1, 2, 3, 4, and 5.

As suit numbers are played, the lead-back numbers are reduced. In the following illustration the 4-0 and 6-1 are played on the 6-0. The 4 is no longer a lead-back number to the blank and the 1 is no longer a lead-back number to the 6. There are now only four lead-back numbers to the 6, the 2, 3, 4, and 5, and four to the blank, the 1, 2, 3, and 5.

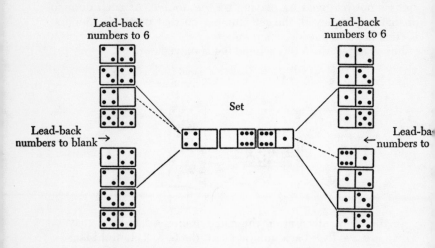

RECURRENCE OF LEAD-BACK NUMBERS

Each of the *suit numbers* on the six singles of a particular suit *remain lead-back numbers so long as the dominoes of that suit are not played*, regardless of whether or not a lead-back number is cut off.

There are five dominoes that can put up a lead-back number for each suit number. There are many possible combinations for a playback that will put up a lead-back number. Remember, a lead-back number is eliminated only when a singles domino of the suit is played. As long as that suit number is not played and all of the five playback dominoes have not been used, it is possible to put up a lead-back number. For example, you hold the 6-1. The 6-0 is set which is followed by a series of plays off of the blank.

Set

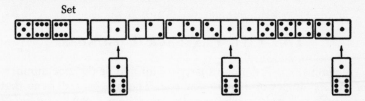

The lead-back number for your 1-6 came up three times on one simple line, starting with the 6-0. The genealogy of the suit number is like a large family tree and branches out in many directions. The occurrences of the 1 in the illustration are only a few of the many possible combinations off of the 6-0 that will lead back to a 1.

It is not always important that a playback be made immediately, but when several rounds have been played and it comes your turn to play, then comes a time to play a lead-back number and help your partner or cut off and hurt your opponent.

HOW TO FIND THE LEAD-BACK NUMBERS

It is easy to find the lead-back numbers by going over the suit numbers and determining the ones that are missing. The missing suit numbers are the lead-back numbers.

For example: The following dominoes were played and you want to know the lead-back numbers available for the 6. You run through the suit numbers, 5 down through blank, affixed to the 6's.

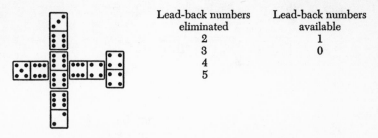

Lead-back numbers eliminated	Lead-back numbers available
2	1
3	0
4	
5	

In the above illustration any domino that will put up a 1 or blank is a playback. The 1 and 0 are lead-back numbers for the 6-1 and 6-0.

THE FIVE PLAYBACK DOMINOES

A playback is a domino that puts up one of the suit numbers of the six singles of a particular suit. The playback domino that puts up a suit or lead-back number must be a *domino of another suit*. The playback domino is the connecting link. Let's take the 6-5 of the 6 suit.

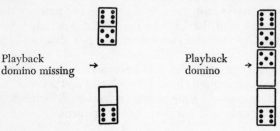

Playback
domino missing →

Playback
domino →

In the above illustration the 5-0 is a playback domino. The 6-0 is a suit domino and cannot lead back to its own suit. The same would be true of the 6-1, 6-2, 6-3, and 6-4.

A playback is made by playing a singles domino on another singles domino and it puts up a suit number that has not been played, frequently called a "new number."

For example: North set the 6-6. The 6 is his suit. East played the 6-3, South the 6-2, and West the 3-5 off of the 3. The 5 is a lead-back number as the 6-5 has not been played.

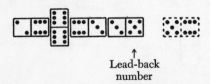

↑
Lead-back
number

A double cannot put up a lead-back number and is not a playback domino but a double can perpetuate a lead-back number if the particular domino of the suit has not been played.

For example: North set the 6-4, East played the 6-2, South the 2-1, and West the 1-1.

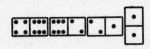

The 1 of the 4 and 6 suits have not been played and the 1 leads back to the 1-6 and 1-4. The 1-1 perpetuates the lead-back number 1.

The playback domino for a particular lead-back number is not limited to one domino. There are five playback dominoes for *each of the six suit numbers* on the singles. Any of five singles dominoes of each of the seven suits having the lead-back number may put it up. In the following illustration the 5-0, 1-0, 2-0, 3-0, and 4-0 are playbacks for the 6-0.

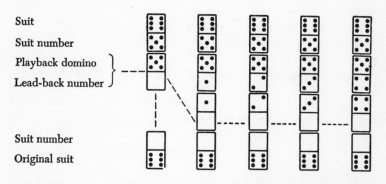

Suit

Suit number

Playback domino }

Lead-back number

Suit number

Original suit

The illustrations above are only five ways of putting up a lead-back number for the 6-0. There are many other combinations for playing playback dominoes and putting up a particular lead-back number.

HOW TO USE THE PLAYBACK

When you have learned all of the other skills in playing the game of dominoes and they become second nature, you should concentrate on the playback. It is the big pay-off play. The playback is used in both offensive and defensive plays.

FIVE WAYS TO USE THE PLAYBACK

There are five important things you can do with the playback when you have the right domino in your hand:

1. *Give your partner a play with a domino of his suit even though you cannot put up that particular number.*

It frequently occurs that your opponents have cut off your partner's numbers or you have been forced to play and cut him off, or you cut him off to take a big score. A playback may give him the number he needs.

2. *Give your partner a lead back to a scoring play.*

When your partner has established and pushed 5's, you can put up a lead-back number to the other 5's and enable him to score when it comes his turn to play.

3. *Cut off a lead-back number that gives your opponent a playback.*

When your opponents put up a lead-back number to their suit it can be cut off to prevent them from playing or controlling the game.

4. *Avoid putting up a lead-back number that gives your opponent control.*

A playback for an opponent's number may give him control and prove very costly to your team. You can usually avoid this by checking the lead-back numbers.

5. *Avoid putting up a lead-back number that gives your opponent a scoring play.*

When your opponent to your right scored and you cannot kick or repeat his score you can frequently avoid giving the next player a lead back to a scoring play. This can save your team many points.

HOW A NUMBER IS ESTABLISHED

In each hand each team or player has one or more long suits in his hands. These are the suits or numbers they wish to establish. In playing cards a player establishes his suit by declaring it. In dominoes, the player identifies a number as his suit by the time, place, and manner in which it is played. For example, a double set is considered the setter's suit or number. If a singles domino is set, the two numbers are his suits or numbers.

When a player sets a double, the odds are 5 to 1 he has at least one more of that number in his hand. When a player sets a singles and he has no double in his hand, the odds are 39 to 1 he has at least one more of each of the two numbers. The numbers set presumably are his long suits.

A suit may also be a particular number that a player has endeavored to establish, as the player on second set, or it may be any number a player has endeavored to establish for scoring, as a 5.

For example: West had the choice of playing his 5-3 off of the 5 or on the 3. He chose to play it on the 3, making both ends 5. Presumably West is long on 5's and wants to establish 5's.

West establishes 5's as his long suit.

In the above illustration North could be in trouble even though he has a play on the 5. When it comes South's turn to play he should give North, his partner, a 6 or blank if possible. However, South may not be able to put up a 6 or blank. In this event he should give North a playback with a number that will lead to a play with a domino of the 6 or blank suit.

HOW TO PUT UP A LEAD-BACK NUMBER

A lead-back number is given by putting up one of the suit numbers that has not been played (frequently called a "new" number). You would deliberately put up a lead-back number for your partner only.

Let's see how this works out. Your partner set the 6-6 and on his second play he played off of his double. The next player played a double on his original play and it is now your turn to play. It is impossible for you to play a domino that will put up a 6, so you check the 6 suit to find out the lead-back numbers. The 0 and 1 are the lead-back numbers.

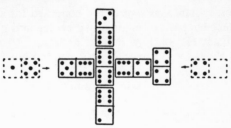

You know there are eight dominoes that will put up a lead-back number for your partner (5-1, 5-0, 3-1, 3-0, 4-1, 4-0, 2-1, and 2-0). You look at your hand and you have a choice of playing the 5-1, 4-3, or 4-0. The 5-1 and 4-0 are playbacks and give your partner a lead-back number. The 4-0 will score 2 points, so you play the 4-0, which scores and gives your partner a "new" or lead-back number. If it should be that your partner has two more 6's in his hand, he will be very glad to get a chance to put up another 6 and set his hand for a sure out.

It is true your opponent can play on the blank and cut it off with the 0-2, 0-3, and 0-5, but this is the chance you have to take. If you played the 5-1 on the 5, your opponent could cut it off with the 1-2, 1-3, and 1-4 and you would be passing up the two points.

HOW TO PERPETUATE A LEAD-BACK NUMBER

A lead-back number is perpetuated by playing a double.

In the following illustration North set the 6-6 and South played the 2-2, which perpetuates the lead-back number 2 for the 6-2.

2-2 perpetuates lead back to 6-2.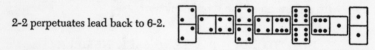

When your team is "on set," all the doubles possible should be played. When your opponents are "on set," you should avoid playing doubles, particularly those that cross a lead-back number.

HOW TO AVOID PUTTING UP A LEAD-BACK NUMBER

A lead-back number is one of the suit numbers that has not been played. You would not deliberately put up a lead-back number for your opponents to their suits or numbers.

Here is a typical example of a playback to the opponents that proved very costly.

Bill was on set and was sent to the boneyard for a load. It happened because his partner made a bad choice and gave his opponent a playback. Here is how it came about.

North set the 6-4 and it was South's turn to play. South had the choice of playing the 1-0 or 1-5.

South played the 1-5, thinking he was putting up a new number for North, his partner, without realizing that it was a playback to a 3 (his opponent's number) with the 5-3.

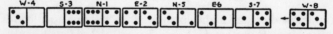

West had the 5-3 and played it off of the 5, making both ends 3's. There were only three dominoes that would play, the 6-3, 3-3, and 3-1 on one number only. North had no 3 in his hand and was forced to the boneyard and off set. This did not have to happen.

If South had played the 1-0, West could not make all of the

ends 3's because the 0-3 had already been played. If West did play off of the 0, he would have to put up the 0-0 or a new number that would lead back to North's 6 or 4 or both, which are his original numbers, plus other possible plays.

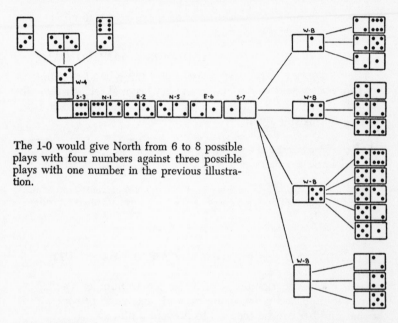

The 1-0 would give North from 6 to 8 possible plays with four numbers against three possible plays with one number in the previous illustration.

A playback can work for or against your team and it can be a decisive play. Now we realize how important the proper choice of plays can be. In the illustration, South's choice played into his opponents' hands, whereas the other choice would have forced the opponents to put up a number that would give his partner a play with one of the dominoes of his 6 or 4 suit.

If you want to play a skillful game of dominoes you must learn the playback technique and then use it when you are playing.

HOW TO CUT OFF A LEAD-BACK NUMBER

There is no set rule about cutting off lead-back numbers for your opponents' suits or numbers. The decision rests primarily on which team is on set. If your partner is on set, he may need that particular number. In this case you would do everything possible to keep numbers open and not cut them off. If your opponents are on set, the lead-back number is not too important to your partner and should be cut off.

There are two simple things to keep in mind in combating the playback:

First, cut off any "new" suit number.

Second, do not put up a double on a lead-back number. This perpetuates the lead-back number.

THE PLAYBACK IN TWO- AND THREE-HANDED GAMES

The playback can be used in two- and three-handed games to give yourself a lead-back number to your original set. It is equally important to avoid a playback and prevent your opponent from putting up his suit again.

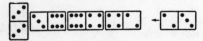 

4-2 puts up lead-back number and permits turning all open numbers into original suit.

4-4 prevents turning all open numbers into original suit.

How to Control a Particular Suit

How the seven dominoes of a particular number (suit) are played is important when that number is needed to provide a play or that number can be blocked to prevent a play.

The important thing to remember is that a particular number can be blocked with the sixth singles domino of that particular number. The double does not block, even though it may be the final play.

SIX OF A PARTICULAR NUMBER PLAYED

When six dominoes of a particular number have been played the seventh of that number can become an unplayable orphan if it is a double. This happens when all of the *singles* dominoes of a particular number have been played and none are left open. The six singles can be matched, leaving none that can be played on. Regardless of which player set, the double can be made an orphan, but a singles cannot. If one or more dominoes with the particular number remain in the boneyard, a double in a player's hand cannot be made an orphan because the particular number may later be drawn.

When the *double has been set or played* it is impossible to have an orphan because the double provides four plays and eight dominoes will lead back to the particular number. For instance, the 2-2 was set.

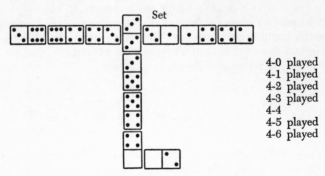

Played	Unplayed	Lead-back Dominoes
2-1	2-3	1-0 for 0-2
2-2	2-0	4-0 " "
2-4		5-0 " "
2-5		6-0 " "
2-6		1-3 for 3-2
		4-3 " "
		5-3 " "
		6-3 " "

When a *singles has been set or played* and six of one of its number have been played, the double of that number is unplayable and becomes an orphan if none of that number are open. A double in your hand that is an orphan means you will be unable to go out and you may have to go to the boneyard and draw. This may result in the opponents getting rid of a lot of dominoes, scoring, and going out. This is a very disastrous and frustrating situation in the game of dominoes. For example, a 3-1 set:

	4-0	played
	4-1	played
	4-2	played
	4-3	played
	4-4	
	4-5	played
	4-6	played

In the above example the player holding the 4-4 is unable to play it, as all of the other 4's have been covered.

FIVE OF A PARTICULAR NUMBER PLAYED

When five dominoes of a particular number have been played, the sixth domino of that number is a very important one to hold. The sixth is the key domino. With the sixth one you can protect

your hand or your partner's hand by playing the sixth so that two
of that number will remain open and the double cannot be cut off,
or, if the double has been played, the sixth number can be kept
open by putting it up so that the number cannot be cut off. On the
other hand, you can cut off the fifth number and prevent the
seventh from playing if it is a double. The way the sixth domino
is played is very important to the player who holds the double.

Example: Protecting the seventh single:

4-4 set.
Five 4's played.

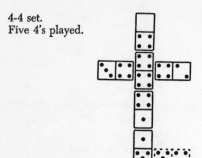

Protecting the hand with the sixth 4
for a sure play with the seventh
domino. The 4-6 cannot be cut off.

Example: Playing the double:

To prevent the double being made an unplayable orphan, it
must be played when the fifth of that number is played unless you
have the sixth of that number. This makes it inadvisable to hold
a double if five of that number have been played and that number
can be cut off by one of the other players.

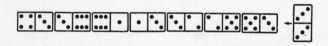

Example: Protecting the double with play off of another double:

Frequently it is possible to avoid playing a double and giving
the opponent a chance of making a large score and yet protect
your hand by playing off of another double and putting up your
doubles *number*. For example, you hold the 4-4 and 6-4, and it is
your turn to play. To play the double on the 4 would give your
opponent a chance to count 25 with the 4-5 or 20 with the 4-0,
so you play the 6-4 on the 6-6 and give your opponent only one
chance to count 10 with the 4-2 for a score of 2 points and still
keep the 4's open for yourself.

Wrong   Right

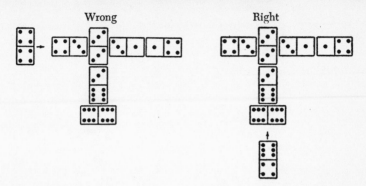

Example: Protecting the double with play off of a single:

3-1 set.
Five 3's played.

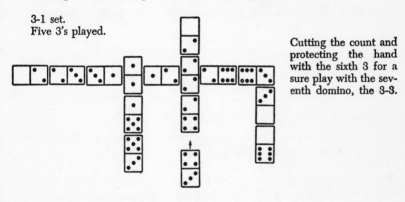

Cutting the count and protecting the hand with the sixth 3 for a sure play with the seventh domino, the 3-3.

Example: Blocking the double:

4-6 set.
Five 4's played.

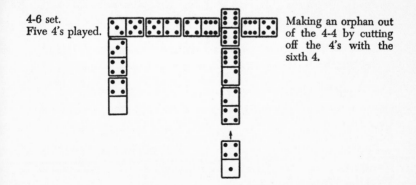

Making an orphan out of the 4-4 by cutting off the 4's with the sixth 4.

PART 6

Making Your Choice of Plays

Favorable Percentage

It is a general law in all games of chance that you should never do a thing or make a choice that you are not willing to repeat under the same circumstances a hundred times.

Five-up is a game of chance (luck) and skill. The possible combinations are astronomical and give the game the element of uncertainty, fun, and flavor.

Five-up differs from games in which there is the element of chance only. In dominoes, skill is equally important as chance, and it is in this respect that it differs from mathematical games of chance such as roulette and dice. Those are strictly gambling games where the player wins when the favorable event happens, as when the number selected by the player comes up, and he loses when the unfavorable occur.

Five-up is unlike games in which there is no element of luck whatsoever. Chance (luck) plays an important part in Five-up and it is in this respect that it differs from games of pure skill such as chess and checkers. Those are games in which the player with superior knowledge of the game has all of the advantages.

In the game of dominoes, all of the players have an equal chance when they draw their original hand of dominoes. There is no skill in drawing because it is merely a matter of chance as to which dominoes are drawn, and nothing is determined until the dominoes are played. However, once the players have drawn their hands they have a choice of which domino they wish to play and a choice of when, where, and how they choose to play it. It is this player's choice that makes dominoes a game of chance and skill.

THE PROBLEM

The only decisions you can make in the entire game are *which* domino you will play and *where* you will play it. Yet when the moment of decision comes and you have a choice of plays, the problem can be very confusing.

In each play you must decide in your own mind your principal objective. Do you want to score, help your partner, tighten the game, open up the game, send the opponents to the boneyard, force the opponents to give you a new number, avoid a possible skunk, assure going out, or prevent your opponent from playing or scoring?

Naturally you would like to do several of these things as score, force your opponent to the boneyard, and go out on the hand. However, rarely can you do all of them, and more often than not you must decide which is the most important to you.

HOW TO SIMPLIFY THE PROBLEM

A simple formula, built by research and experience, provides a logical and open-minded approach to the problem. It does not guarantee finding the right solution every time. What it does is to overcome the temptation to arrive at snap judgments and helps avoid costly errors. Use it and you'll have a high batting average.

Identify the Problem

The first essential step is to pinpoint the problem which you may be able to do something about.

Set position—Ordinarily, going out on the hand is the main objective of the team on set. If you or your partner are on set and going out is your prime objective, you will play an open and scoring game. On the other hand, if the odds favor scoring or forcing your opponents to the boneyard, you may decide to score or force your opponents to the boneyard and take a chance on going out.

If your opponents are on set, ordinarily the odds are in favor of scoring. However, if you or your partner have gone to the boneyard for a load, the odds may be in favor of forcing your opponents off set.

Scoreboard—If you are way ahead on the scoreboard you may decide to play conservatively, keep the scoring low, and maintain your lead. In this case you play an open game—give a little and take a little—to assure winning. On the other hand, if you are way behind you may decide to tighten the game, hoping to force your opponent to the boneyard and catch him with a large count, or you may decide to build up the count and try for some big scores to overcome your opponent's lead. In these circumstances you are mainly interested in the possibility of winning the game, and your position on the scoreboard is the prime factor that determines your strategy.

EVALUATE YOUR FACTS

The second phase is to consider all the information that has a bearing on your problem. Don't settle for an assumption on any point where it is possible to obtain facts and figures.

Table—The dominoes on the table convey valuable information. By counting the dominoes of each suit you can determine the odds against your opponent having a playable domino. By checking the suit numbers you can determine the scoring dominoes that may be held by your opponents. A complete explanation of suit count is given in Part 5—"How to Master Suit Control."

By observing carefully the plays made—who, what, and how— you should have gained much information about your partner's and opponents' suits and strategy. A detailed explanation on the evaluation of plays is given in Part 4—"How to Evaluate Specific Plays."

These two things—suit control and information gained during play—are invaluable in deciding your strategy.

Your hand—How your hand fits in with the dominoes played and your partner's strategy mean a lot in deciding your strategy. Ordinarily if you hold good scoring dominoes, kickers and re-peaters, you can afford to score and build up the count. If you have a poor hand, ordinarily the odds favor reducing the count. Of course there are many other considerations and they are covered elsewhere.

SELECT THE BEST PLAY

This is the area of decision. Occasionally one clearly superior solution will stand out. But often it is not that simple. In this situa-tion put *favorable percentage* into action. This is the guiding factor that will help you make *the right play at the right time*. It is the basis of all the principles of plays set forth in this book.

Consciously or unconsciously, all correct plays are based on favorable percentage. Plays based on a hunch or speculation buck-ing the odds may work out occasionally, but in the long run such plays will prove disastrous and result in lost games.

Playing favorable percentage means doing the thing or making the choice that gives you the best odds in the circumstances that confront you. Remember, favorable percentage is not certainty, and a number of plays are bound to go against you in spite of the percentage in your favor. Even though some of your plays have not worked out well and there has been a run of luck against you, do not throw away your principle of playing favorable percentage. *Stick with favorable percentage* and accept the results philosophically.

In actual play it is not practical or necessary that you determine the exact odds on each play, but it is important that you make the choice that gives you the best odds.

Player's Chances—Original Five Draw

"The probable is that which usually happens."—ARISTOTLE

The odds on each play involve two situations; first, the odds against a player *holding* a particular number or a particular domino in the draw of the *original hand* of five dominoes; and, second, the odds of a player *drawing* a particular number or a particular domino when the player is forced to draw *from the boneyard*.

ORIGINAL FIVE DRAW

There are 98,280 possible hands, and when you or any other player draws five dominoes there is no way of telling which numbers or dominoes the other player holds. However, each player's *chances* of drawing matching numbers, different numbers, a particular domino, and a particular number or doubles have been determined and are used as the bases of the plays set forth. The most important ones are given in various sections of the book.

The probabilities are set forth in simple terms and are easily understood. They are shown in terms of the number of favorable chances out of 100, except when this is not convenient or practical. All numbers have been rounded off to the nearest whole number. It should be remembered that 50 out of 100 is the equivalent of even odds, or 1 to 1. Thus 75 times out of 100 is 3 to 1, 80 times out of 100 is 4 to 1, etc.

The algebraic calculations to determine these probabilities are probably not of interest to the average reader, and therefore have been omitted. The calculations, methods, and principles applied have been checked by competent mathematicians.

DRAWING ONE PARTICULAR DOMINO— ORIGINAL DRAW

There are twenty-eight dominoes in the deck. Each player, whether 1, 2, 3, or 4, draws his hand of five dominoes. What is each player's chance of drawing one *particular domino,* say the 6-3?

Regardless of the order of drawing, the odds are the same for each player and for each domino such as the 6-3, 5-5, or 4-1, etc.

Before looking at your hand the chances *against drawing one particular domino* are 5 chances in 28:

> 28 chances
> 5 favorable
> ———
> 23 unfavorable—odds 4.60 to 1 against

After looking at your hand you learn that you did not draw a particular domino, say the 6-3. The chances of each of the other players having drawn this particular domino are now greater. Their individual chances are 5 chances in 23:

> 23 chances
> 5 favorable
> ———
> 18 unfavorable—odds 3.60 to 1 against

These odds are determined by simple arithmetic.

PLAYER'S CHANCES—DRAWING FROM BONEYARD

When you are in a position to force your opponent to draw from the boneyard, how can you determine the odds against your opponent drawing a particular number or a particular domino? What are your chances if you are forced to draw?

Knowing these odds may be very important in a particular play. It helps to decide when it is wise to force the opponent to draw from the boneyard. Also, it helps to decide when it is smart to pass up points and keep solvent instead of scoring and speculating on the possibility of your being forced to draw from the boneyard. Your decision should be based on favorable odds, not on hunches.

We are concerned here with the odds against *drawing* a particular domino or a particular number *from the boneyard.*

SIMPLE ARITHMETIC

The odds against the player who is forced to draw from the boneyard is made by simple arithmetic in each situation. There is no predetermined schedule of odds.

To arrive at the correct odds we must know first whether we are considering the chances of drawing one *particular domino*, say the 6-1, or one *particular number*, say any 4. Next, we determine the total possibilities and then we determine the favorable possibilities. The odds are determined from these two figures.

1. Total possibilities. This is the total number of dominoes in which the particular domino or the particular numbers are included. We know the dominoes in our hand and can exclude the dominoes in the hand of the player forced to draw. Thus the dominoes with the needed number or the particular domino are in the boneyard or in the other two players' hands. The total of these is our total possibilities.

2. Favorable possibilities. This is the number of dominoes with the needed number which are unaccounted for. For example: If four 3's have been played or accounted for it would leave three favorable possibilities. In the case of one particular domino the favorable possibility is merely one.

3. Unfavorable possibilities. Having determined the total possibilities, we deduct the favorable possibilities and determine the unfavorable possibilities. The odds are determined as follows:

$$\begin{array}{r} 18 \text{ possibilities} \\ \underline{3} \text{ favorable} \\ 15 \text{ unfavorable—15 to 3—odds 5 to 1 against.} \end{array}$$

The expectancy is 17 times out of 100.

KNOWLEDGE GAINED DURING PLAY INCREASES ACCURACY

The odds against a player drawing from the boneyard are based upon the total possibilities. Any information you may have gained during the play of the hand enables you to reduce the total possibilities and arrive at truer odds.

For example: If you know the 6-3 is not in any of the players' hands, then it must be among the dominoes in the boneyard. If there were two dominoes in the boneyard and a player is forced to draw, the odds would be 1 to 1 against his drawing the 6-3. On the other hand, if the 6-3 could be in two players' hands, who hold seven dominoes, or in the two dominoes in the boneyard, the odds against the player forced to draw would be 8 to 1 against him.

This knowledge is gained by watching the numbers or dominoes played by your partner and your opponents.

For example: In a previous play you played the 3-3, and scored 3 points. Your opponent to your left followed with the 2-1. If your opponent had the 6-3 he surely would have played it off the 3-3 for a score of 3 points instead of playing the 2-1 off of the 2-2. Thus you know this opponent does not hold the 6-3 in his hand. The dominoes in his hand may be discarded in determining the total possibilities and odds against another player drawing this particular domino.

The same principle that applies to a particular domino such as the 6-3 also applies to particular numbers like any 4.

How to Figure Odds of Player Drawing One Particular Domino (from Boneyard)

The odds against drawing a particular domino are simply the unfavorable possibilities to 1.

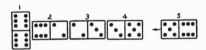

The unfavorable possibilities are the total possibilities less the favorable possibilities which, in this case, is 1. To determine the total possibilities, count the dominoes in the other players' hands (do not count those in your hand and those in the hand of the player drawing) and add this to the number of dominoes in the boneyard.

For example: It is your second play and you can send East, your opponent to your left, to the boneyard, as he was unable to play on his first play. What are East's chances of drawing the 6-3?

There are two players, South and West, who may be holding the particular domino, the 6-3, and they each have four dominoes. There are six in the boneyard. There are 14 possibilities, 13 unfavorable and 1 favorable. The odds against East drawing the particular domino (6-3) are 13 to 1. After each unsuccessful draw the odds are reduced to 12 to 1, 11 to 1, etc.

If there were two particular dominoes desired, say the 6-1 or 5-5, the odds are the number of unfavorable chances to the number of favorable chances (desired dominoes), which, in this case, is two.

How to Figure Odds of Player Drawing One Particular Number (from Boneyard)

The odds against *any player* drawing one particular number are always the unfavorable possibilities to the favorable possibilities.

To determine the total possibilities, count the dominoes in the other players' hands (do not count those in your hand and those in the hand of the player drawing), and add this to the number of dominoes in the boneyard. This is the total number of favorable and unfavorable possibilities. Next, determine how many of the particular number have been played (plus those in your hand), and deduct this number from the seven pieces of that number in the full deck. The difference is the number of dominoes unaccounted for, which is the number of favorable ways the number can be drawn. Subtract the favorable ways from the total possibilities and you have the number of unfavorable ways. Let us take a look at a few illlustrations.

Opponent draws—four-handed game: Your opponent is unable to play and needs a 2. Four 2's have been played and three are unaccounted for. There are three favorable possibilities. The two other players hold seven dominoes and six dominoes remain in the boneyard. The total possibilities are 13. The odds on the first draw are:

13 chances
3 favorable
10 unfavorable—10 to 3—odds 3.33 to 1 against opponent

The expectancy is 23 times out of 100.

After each unsuccessful draw the total possibilities are reduced 1, thus reducing the odds to 3.00 to 1, 2.67 to 1, 2.33 to 1, 2.00 to 1, and 1.67 to 1 on the sixth draw.

You draw—four-handed game: Three 6's have been played. You have none and are forced to draw. Seven dominoes are in your opponents' and partner's hands with eight dominoes remaining in the boneyard. The total possibilities are 15. There are four

6's unaccounted for in the other players' hands or in the boneyard. Thus there are four favorable chances. The odds on the first draw are:

15 chances
 4 favorable
───
11 unfavorable—11 to 4—odds 2.75 to 1 against you

Your expectancy is 27 times out of 100

Opponent draws—two-handed game: Three 5's have been played and you hold two more 5's. There are ten dominoes left in the boneyard. Two are 5's. Your opponent is unable to play and is forced to draw. What are the odds against your opponent drawing a 5? The odds are:

10 chances
 2 favorable
───
 8 unfavorable—8 to 2—odds 4 to 1 against opponent

Your opponent's expectancy is 20 times out of 100.

PART 7

Lessons

Lesson No. 1—Basic Strategy, Four-handed Game

The four-handed Five-up game can be played automatically or you can apply a great deal of skill. At first, while learning the game, don't worry about your plays. Beginner's luck will take care of you. As you continue to play you will see the many possibilities for making astute plays and you will learn to use them to your advantage.

MAKE TEAMWORK YOUR GUIDE

Teamwork is the keynote of partnership play in a four-handed game. In every sport, business enterprise, or joint venture the partners, to be successful, must coordinate their efforts and help each other. They must work or play together in harmony and not against each other. This is true in every phase of life and it is equally true in the four-handed game of dominoes. The partners must play as a team to get the best results out of the dominoes in their hands.

Conveying correct information to your partner by your plays is one of the important skills in the four-handed game. By your play you can indicate the number you want and your strategy, or both. You may indicate that you prefer to reduce the count or that you want to build up the count or that you want to tighten the game or open it up. However, no information may be conveyed by remarks or comments or by sign, as by crossing a number with the hand to suggest that a double be played. Such information is improper and unsportsmanlike.

BELIEVE YOUR PARTNER

You must watch your partner's plays carefully. By carefully watching the numbers put up or cut off by your partner and your opponents valuable information is gained and helpful conclusions, deductions, or assumptions may be made. The correct interpretation of your partner's and opponents' play is essential to your choice of play. You must back up your partner by supporting his play and he, in turn, must help you. For two partners to play for themselves is like two horses pulling in opposite directions and going nowhere.

KNOW WHO IS ON SET

The term "on set" is always used to designate the player who is presently in the position to play his last domino first and go out on the hand. This is the preferred position and the key to all plays.

To make the right plays and help your partner you *must keep in mind at all times which player is on set.* If the player on original set goes off set, then both the teams' and players' strategy changes. To play and then ask, "Who is on set?" is as ludicrous as to ask, "What is trump?" in a game of bridge. Dominoes is similar to the game of football. Each player must know which team and which player has the ball in order to play his part. When a team loses the ball, *the entire strategy changes.* The same principle applies to dominoes.

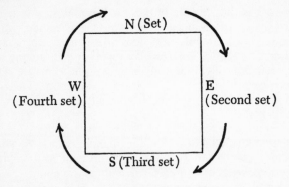

KNOW YOUR OBJECTIVE

The objective of each team and the strategy of each player depend upon which team is on set.

Partners on set are the offensive team. Their objective is to score and go out on their hand. The opponents are the defensive team. Their objective is to score and force their opponents off set if possible.

The partners of each team must coordinate their strategy if they hope to achieve their objective. Yet each player's part differs from that of his partner and from that of the other players. Each player's strategy depends upon his playing position in relation to the player on set. North, the player on set, is the head of his team and calls the plays. He stays in this position throughout the hand unless he goes off set. This is fundamental. This principle is violated by some partners when they have a wonderful hand, say four 5's, and they decide to take a gamble. They will take over and score like mad, even though they may send North, their partner who is on set, to the boneyard. East, who is on second set (second player), is the head of the defensive team and calls the plays but may take the cue given to him by his partner and help force the player on set to the boneyard.

KNOW YOUR JOB

Your playing position changes with each new hand and during the play of a hand if the setter goes off set. If you keep in mind your position in relation to the "set" position, it is fairly easy to know what domino to play and how to play it.

North (on set)

The setter's responsibility is to establish his hand and go out on his set. The set and the partner's first play lay the foundation for the ensuing plays—like the foundation for a house—and it must be solid and it must be right.

The player on set must keep solvent. In general, he should not speculate and score except under favorable or advantageous circumstances.

East (second set)

East's job is to score and establish his own numbers to keep himself in a position to go out if North goes off set. North will go off set approximately one out of four times.

When East has been forced to draw a lot of dominoes he is in a position to control the game and should attempt to do so, relying on his partner to help him.

South (third set)

South's role is to protect his partner from being forced off set. This is done by playing doubles and putting up numbers his partner needs. South should be more concerned with keeping setter on set than scoring or establishing his own numbers. For example, if South has a lot of 4's, he can assume that his partner does not have any and should not try to establish 4's unless he intends to take over control. Should East, who is on second set, go into the boneyard for a lot of dominoes, and South (the setter's partner) can be assured of going out with the dominoes in his hand, in view of the dominoes played, South should then take control and play to assure his going out rather than try to help his partner (setter) who may or may not be able to domino.

West (fourth set)

West is the hatchet man. His job is to go after the setter. If he can force North off set, his partner (East) is on set. West's main objective is to cut off North's numbers and help East, his partner. He takes his cue from his partner's plays—the numbers put up and the numbers cut off. If East, his partner, has been forced to draw from the boneyard, he may be in a position to control the game. West must support his partner and it is his job to get tough rather than attempt to gain control. If North is forced off set and East goes on set, then West's strategy changes immediately and it becomes the same as that indicated for South when North was on set.

DETERMINE YOUR STRENGTH

The first thing you should do when you draw your hand is to determine your longest suit and your kickers and repeaters.

By counting the dominoes played and those in your hand, and watching who played those numbers, you can readily determine who is strong in a particular suit and who is weak. This information is invaluable in all your plays.

If the dominoes of each suit were distributed evenly among four players and the boneyard, each player could expect to hold one suit with two or three dominoes of that number. In the original draw of five dominoes, the chances of drawing two or more matching numbers are 998 out of 1,000, and 3 or more, 53 out of 100.

When you have only one of a number you are weak in that suit, and you have an average suit when you have two. Three or more of a particular number is a strong suit. If you hold three dominoes of a particular number, say 5's, then there can only be four left in the other players' hands and in the boneyard. If your partner is on set, it is obvious he probably is short on 5's unless he indicated he has 5's by putting them up. The same is true of your opponents.

How you play your longest suit depends upon who is on set and your position in relation to the set. If your partner is on set, you would not try to establish your longest suit, as it would only help send him to the boneyard. On the other hand, if the player to your left is on set, you would establish and push your longest suit.

Cutting off or putting up numbers is one of the important strategis. In the early part of a hand many astute players do not put up a singles number needed by their partner on set because the opponents will probably cut it off. So they frequently put up a different number and, in this way, let their opponents cut it off and put up the number needed.

PLAY AN OPEN GAME

The four-handed game is more of an open and aggressive scoring game than the two-handed. In the four-handed there are twenty dominoes in the players' hands with only eight in the boneyard, while in the two-handed there are only ten in the players' hands and eighteen in the boneyard. In the four-handed game most of the scoring is done on plays rather than the dominoes remaining in the players' hands. By playing an open game it helps keep your team solvent and gives you and your partner an opportunity to score.

Score—A skillful and experienced player will pass up a score and tighten the game to force his opponent to draw if he figures the opponent to his left may hold a good repeater or kicker such as the 5-5, but these situations are relatively infrequent. Remember, this is a scoring game and points should not be passed up unless it serves some good purpose.

Make kickers and repeaters pay off—Your kickers and repeaters are the best scoring dominoes. They must not be wasted, but held, as they will prove very profitable when the scoring starts. Ordinarily the 6-1 and 5-0 should not be played for the sake of one point. They should be held for a possible score of 3 or more points. The 5-5 is an excellent kicker and, ordinarily, should be held, as 5's usually come up.

Keep solvent—Next to scoring, the most important thing is to keep your team out of the boneyard. This means you must think of your partner as well as yourself and make it a partnership game.

LESSON NO. 2—FIRST ROUND, TEAM ON ORIGINAL SET AND A, B, AND C SYSTEMS OF PLAY

The objective of the team on original set is to score during play and go out on the hand, scoring the count in the opponents' hands. Your team is in first position to go out and the setter has the choice of set. This gives you the advantage.

It is very important for the setter to retain his set position and go out on the hand. To go out means your team receives the count in your opponents' hands, whereas if your team fails to go out, your opponents receive the count in your hands. The difference between going out and not going out can add up to many points.

The team in second set position can go out only if they can force the player on set off of his set position. If North is forced off set, then East is on set, and if he is forced to draw, then South, and so on.

To profit from his advantage the player on original set must set the domino that gives him the most favorable odds and that conveys correct information to his partner.

CONVEYING INFORMATION TO PARTNER

The player on set needs his partner's help, and his opening play should give his partner a clue to the setter's hand on which his partner will base his plays if he has a choice.

The set must convey correct information to the partner. To misinform the partner may prove disastrous to a good hand and result in a lost game. The partner, in turn, must accept the information conveyed by the set as being correct and help his partner, if possible, by making the right plays. Failure to support his partner may cause him to go off set. This may result in a "minus set" for the hand, which means he lost his advantage and made less points on the hand than the opponents made. To assure going out the team on set must work together in harmony.

The principal difficulty that domino players encounter in a four-handed game is the different concepts in the choice of play by the player on set and his partner's first play. A player's view or method may have been adopted through experience gained in years of playing dominoes, or from playing with a certain group of players. Many have no definite plan and play as their mood dictates at the moment. As a result, the set may convey incorrect information or no information. The partner may make a choice of play which spoils his partner's hand and throw away many favorable possibilities.

In the game of contract bridge there have been developed several excellent systems by which correct information may be conveyed to the partner. This enables the players to get the most out of their hands. In dominoes there has never been published a system for partnership play. As a result, too many players have no system. Many play by domino sense developed through experience, but this can be very confusing. In playing with different players, we find different ideas of play and frequently unsound ideas of play are adopted and followed. Thus, when a decision to make a play works out well, it was a great play. If it did not work, it was a dumb play. Yet too frequently a good play made by a player does not work out favorably because the partner's play was not compatible or coordinated to his play.

THREE SYSTEMS

A survey was made of the methods of play used by many experienced and skillful players. Their various ideas were tabulated and reduced down to three distinct systems. Each has its merit. Players who follow any one of them have a distinct advantage over players who have no system. This does not mean that players who follow a system are sure to win a hand or the game. There are so many possible hands in dominoes that there can be no system of play that will assure winning. If there were such a system, dominoes would no longer be a competitive game. Nor is it improper to use a system of play. It is one of the skills of the game just as informatory bids are in the game of bridge. The important thing about a system of play in dominoes is that it enables the team on set to coordinate their play insofar as the dominoes in their hands provide a choice.

The three systems are designated A, B, and C games. Once these methods of play become known, two players can readily indicate what system they will use and then play accordingly. If your partner does not follow one of these three systems, you may be able to determine how he plays the game by one or two simple questions or by playing with him. In this case you should adapt yourself to his style. Once you are familiar with the A, B, and C systems you can adjust your method of play easily. In any event, adopt one particular system and follow it until you find it necessary to adapt your play to your partner's system or ideas.

There are two principal differences in the three systems. One concerns the first domino played by the player on set. The second is on the partner's response. Some players will not set a lighthouse, and some partners consider it almost a crime if their partner sets a lighthouse. Others prefer to set a lighthouse and get rid of it. Some players will play off of their partner's double set. Others prefer to leave it alone. Some players insist that their partner play off of their double set. Many players will only set a singles domino that they can play off of both ends and resist the temptation to score. Others will play the 6-4, 4-1, or 0-5, and take the count. These differences of opinion are what make the game interesting. Yet it is readily apparent that two persons playing as partners can play a much better game by following the same system, whatever it may be.

The basic principles of the three systems apply to the team on set in the first round of the hand only. They are explained in detail in this lesson. The general principles that apply to the opponents' team in the first round and to both teams in the second and subsequent rounds are treated in the next two lessons.

GENERAL PRINCIPLES FOR SETTING A, B, OR C SYSTEMS

Remember, the objective of the team on set is to score and go out. Regardless of the theory or system followed, the objective is the same.

If the player on set does not have to make a choice between setting a lighthouse or a singles with two different numbers, the correct set is based on favorable percentage and is the same regardless of the system one follows. Sets are listed below in the order of the most favorable odds for the team on set.

Setting Doubles

1. If you have a double and one or more dominoes with the same number, set the double.

   If you have two or more doubles, set the double of your longest suit. You have 6-6, 6-1, 4-4, 4-3, 4-1. Set the 4-4.

   If you have two or more doubles, set the large number if you wish to keep the score down, the small number if you want to build up the count.

2. Follow A, B, or C system on setting a lighthouse double.

   If your partner does not make it a practice of crossing (playing on) your set, as a general rule, avoid the lighthouse set and your partner's wrath.

   If you have two or more lighthouse doubles, including the 5-5 or 0-0, hold either of these for scoring later.

3. When you have four dominoes of a suit, including the double, and the fifth is a lighthouse double, set the double of the long suit.

   Exception: If your partner plays the "C" system, set the lighthouse double.

Setting Singles

4. Set a singles domino that gives you most plays off of both ends.

   (a) If you hold a scoring domino on which you cannot play on both ends, you should resist the temptation to play the scoring domino. Set the domino that you can play on both ends unless the score assures your team going out or prevents a "skunk" game. When you set a singles, your partner will assume you have both numbers in your hand and he will be misled if you do not have both numbers.

   (b) If you have a scoring domino on which you can play off of both ends, such as 6-4, 4-1, or 3-2, set the scoring domino. Do not set the 5-0 if you have another domino on which you can play on both ends, as 5's are bound to come up and 5-0 is a good scoring kicker.

   (c) If you cannot score, play a domino that gives your opponent no opportunity to score, or the least chance to score, and the smallest score. This will depend on your hand. You hold 6-3, 4-2, 4-0, 3-1, 1-0. You would not set the 6-3 and give your opponent the opportunity to score 3 points or the 4-2 or 4-0 for a possible 2 points. The best set would be 1-0 as your opponent has one chance only to score 1 point with the 1-5. The 3-1 gives the opponent three chances to score with 1-1, 3-4, or 1-2. The 4-0 gives three chances to score with 0-6, 0-1, and 4-5.

   Do not set the 6-1 if you have another domino on which you can play on both ends, as 6-1 is one of the best scoring dominoes in the deck and will probably come in handy later in the hand.

5. If you do not have a domino that gives you a play on both ends, set the domino that scores, gives you the most plays on one end, or gives your opponent the least chances to score. For example, you hold the 6-4, 6-3, 6-0, 5-2, and 5-1. Set the 6-4.

"A" GAME—AUTHORITATIVE SYSTEM

The "A" game is played by the majority of the domino players. It is based on an old theory that the player on set must never set a lighthouse. This system developed out of the theory that the player on set should play a number he can play on and indicate to his partner the number he has in his hand.

Here are the basic principles of the "A" game:

Setter

1. Set a double, but never a lighthouse.
2. Set a singles with most plays off of both ends.

Partner

1. Cross opponent's number if possible, otherwise play off of opponent's number.

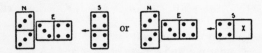

Since you know your partner will not set a lighthouse you are expected to leave your partner's set alone. This tightens up the game for your opponent to your left and gives him only two numbers to play on. It forces him to give your partner on set a new number, play a double, or put up another of your partner's original number.

"B" GAME—BLEND SYSTEM

The "B" game is played by many domino players with good "domino sense." They set the domino that fits in best with the numbers in their hand. This system is more flexible than the "A" or "C" game. It requires much skill and dexterity with a willingness to take chances based on superior knowledge of the game and the ability to diagnose plays and calculate fairly accurately the dominoes that are held in the other players' hands or which remain in the boneyard.

Setter

1. Set a double including a lighthouse if it will encourage and lead to the other numbers in the hand.

Exception: Do not set a lighthouse 5-5.

Since there is no assurance that your partner will cross your set there are several sound reasons for not setting the 5-5 lighthouse. It gives the opponents an opportunity to outscore the team on set and block the setter from playing. For example, North set a lighthouse 5-5 and East plays the 5-0 and scores 2 points. South plays the 0-1 and West plays the 1-5 for 3 points. The opponents scored 5 points against the setter's 2 points and forced the setter off set. When the 5-5 is set, the plays following are attracted to scores with 5s. (This is not true of the 0-0.) Another reason for not setting the 5-5 lighthouse is that it is a good kicker to hold for scoring later when the big scoring is usually done.

2. Set a singles that gives the most plays on both ends.

Partner

1. When your partner sets a double, play off of his double if you have two or more dominoes in your hand with the same number as his set.

2. Cross opponent's number. (Always a good play.)

3. Play off of opponent's number.

"C" GAME—CROSS SYSTEM

The "C" game is presently the minority system, but it is used by some of the most experienced players and consistent winners. It is based on the practice of crossing the setter's or opponent's number. We call it the "Cross System" or "C" game.

The "C" game is based on two major premises—(1) the set shall convey correct information to the partner and (2) the partner shall make the proper responding play. This is not to say that every play by the setter's partner can be predetermined, but rather that this system makes it imperative for the setter's partner to cross a single or a double when he is able to do it. This practice is necessary, as approximately one time out of eight the set will be a lighthouse. If the double set is not a lighthouse, the odds of the setter holding exactly two dominoes that match the set are 2 to 1 against him. The odds against his holding exactly three are 21 to 1. Thus usually the setter will have several different numbers and he needs numbers to play on, which is what the cross system gives him.

The cross system is not based on certainty. There is no infallible system. It is presented as a sound way to play a good four-handed partnership game. It takes advantage of favorable percentage, gives more accurate information to the partner than the "A" or

"B" game, and protects the setter. The cross system is recommended as the most rewarding.

Here are the basic rules of the "C" game.

Setter

1. Set a double, including a lighthouse, if necessary.

   You must set a double if you have one in your hand. Set the double with the longest suit. If you hold one or more doubles, but do not have any matching numbers that will play on the doubles, then set a lighthouse double. Exception: As a general rule do not set the 5-5 or 0-0 lighthouse. If you hold four of one suit, including the double, and a lighthouse double, set the lighthouse. There are several factors in favor of setting a double.

   (a) You get rid of a double.

   (b) A double including a lighthouse provides the setter with the most favorable odds against the second player having a playable or scoring domino. He will go to the boneyard one time out of four. The odds are 3.6 to 1 against his holding a scoring domino, unless the 2-2 is set. Then the odds are 1.5 to 1.

   (c) If the second player is forced to draw, your partner is automatically on second set, which means he is in a position to go out if you should happen to go off set.

   (d) When you set away from your hand by setting a lighthouse double, the other numbers in your hand will usually come up in the course of events. Say you have 6-6, 1-1, 2-0, 4-5, 3-4. Whether you set the 6-6 or 1-1, your opponent must put up a new number. In addition, your partner is bound to give you numbers under this cross system of play.

   (e) Your partner is in a good spot. He will be able to cross your set four times out of five if you set a lighthouse. He will be able to play 97 times out of 100. The probability of your partner going to the boneyard is only 3 times out of 100.

   (f) You score just as many if not more points as opponents.

2. Set singles with most plays on both ends.

   This set informs your partner that you have no double and that you can play on both ends of the domino you set. It establishes the two numbers that fit your hand.

Partner

1. Play off of partner's double if you hold two or more of number set.

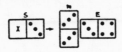

When your partner sets a double, you can expect that he drew two or more of that particular number 80 out of 100 times. It is likely he will have one other domino with the same number as the double he set. The odds are against his holding more than one, and the more dominoes you hold with the same number as the double he set, the less likely he is to have more than one. As the "cross" system requires your partner to set a lighthouse double, it is absolutely essential that you protect him by giving him numbers to play on. *Yours is the key play.* When you have two or more of your partner's double set you must resist the temptation to score. If necessary, pass up 1, 2, or even 3 points and cross his double set. By playing off of his double you give him three numbers to play on. This gives your partner the choice of tightening the game if he should hold several of the number set.

Exception: If East has gone to the boneyard, your main objective is for your team to go out and get the count in your opponents' hands. In this situation you must evaluate your hand and

  (a) if you hold a good hand, play for yourself to go out in the event your partner goes off set or
  (b) if you hold a poor hand, play to your partner's hand and help him to go out.

As a general rule, if East has drawn one, two, three, or four dominoes, cross your partner's set. If East has drawn a load, say five, six, or seven, it is not necessary for you to cross your partner's set on your first play, as West most likely will play off of the set to give his partner numbers to play on. If West does not cross your partner's set, then you should cross it on your next play.

2. Cross opponent's number or play off of partner's double if you hold only one of number set.
   When your turn to play comes you *must cross the domino played by the opponent to your right and get a double up or*

play off of your partner's double. This gives your partner two spinners or three numbers to play on and is a good percentage play because your partner has four dominoes left with seven possible numbers. Let us say your partner set the 4-4 and your opponent to your right played the 4-2. If you have the 2-2 it should be played. If you do not have it, then you should play off of the 4-4. This is a crucial play and you must protect your partner.

If necessary, you should pass up one or two points to give your partner a cross.

Exceptions: (a) If you hold only one of your partner's double set and *you can score three points,* you may take the score.

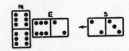

On your second play you must give your partner a cross on his set if no plays have been made on his set (6-6).

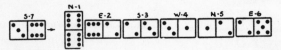

(b) If East has gone to the boneyard your main objective is for your team to go out.

It is not necessary for you (South) to cross your partner's set on your first play, as West will most likely play off of the set to give his partner a play. If West does not cross your partner's set, then you should cross it on your next play.

3. If you have none of partner's double set and cannot cross opponent's number, then score or put up number you have least of in your hand.

When you play off of your opponent's number there is always the possibility that the fourth player may be able to play a domino that will make all of the numbers the same as the double set by your partner. This forces your partner on set to play one of his original numbers or, if he set a lighthouse, to draw from the boneyard.

2-2 set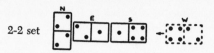

Your best play is to put up the number you have least of in your hand. This gives your partner the best chance to play, particularly if West plays off of the double.

4. If your partner set a singles domino:
   (a) Cross one of his numbers, if possible, or
   (b) Cross opponent's number, if possible, or
   (c) Play off of opponent's number, putting up your partner's original number, if possible.

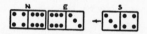

Otherwise, put up the number you have least of in your hand. This gives your partner the best chances to play if West cuts off your partner's original number.

   (d) If you must play off of your partner's number it is impossible to avoid a lead back to opponent's (East's) number. Your best play is to put up the number you have least of in your hand. This gives your partner the best chance to play if West is forced to play off of his partner's number.

LESSON No. 3—FIRST ROUND, OPPONENTS OF TEAM ON ORIGINAL SET AND PARTNER'S PET PEEVE

The opponents of the team on set are in a secondary position.

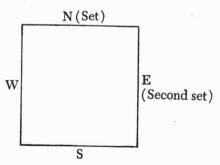

The objective of the team on second set is threefold: *score, keep solvent, force setter off set*.

The strategy of the team on second set is to make aggressive plays that will score, if possible, cut off their opponents' numbers, and establish their own numbers by putting up the ones they have most of.

Scoring points is the *principal objective*. The team on set will frequently pass up points to maintain their set positions. By scoring aggressively you can frequently outscore the team on set and force them to choose between scoring and keeping solvent. In this way you can overcome the points remaining in your hands if the team on set goes out.

The *second objective* is to stay out of the boneyard if possible. This saves many points if North, the player on set, goes out. Then, too, if East stays on second set he could be in a position to go out if North goes off set. The chances of North going off set are approximately 1 out of 4. On the other hand, if East goes to the boneyard, South goes on second set and East's team may be caught with many points left in their hands.

The domino set is the other team's primary number or numbers which they will try to establish, and consequently those numbers are your team's first target. The strategy is to attack and cover their set by playing on the double or cutting off their singles, and to establish your own numbers. Put up the singles numbers that you have the most of in your hand. The more of a particular number you have, the better chance there is of that number holding up. Play doubles on your numbers or your partner's numbers. This provides three more plays on that number.

The *third objective* is to put your team on set. If the player on set can be forced off set, then East goes on set, and this places your team in an advantageous position. If he can then go out, you not only save the points in your hands, but receive the points left in the hands of the team on original set. In the first round of play it is practically impossible to prevent South, the setter's partner, from playing, as there are two numbers open and the player's chances of playing are between 95 and 97 times out of 100. Consequently, at this stage of play it is advantageous to score rather than attempt to force the player to the boneyard.

EAST—SECOND PLAYER
(First Play after Set)

East is the second player and is on second set. He must keep solvent so that he may go out if the player on set is forced to draw and go off set. East's first play is an important one for his team. Here are the basic rules:

Setter Has Set a Double

1. Score, if possible, or

2. If unable to score, play the domino with the number you hold most of in your hand. If you do not score, your partner will assume you like the number you played and will cross it with a double, follow your lead, or, if it is cut off, he will put it up again as soon as possible, or

3. Play the domino that gives opponent the least chance to score or the lowest possible score.

Setter Has Set a Singles

1. Cut off one of the numbers and score, or

2. If unable to score, play number that fits your hand best to play on later or which may help send the opponent to the boneyard.

3. *Do not play a double* because it sets up the number with a spinner and insures the opponents going out. Ordinarily it is better to die with it, unless you have a sticky or poor hand and want to get rid of dominoes and get the hand over with, or you want to keep the play open.

In a four-handed game, twenty out of twenty-eight dominoes are in the players' hands and usually three or more numbers are up on the third or fourth round. It is not so difficult to get rid of doubles in a four-handed game as it is in a two- or three-handed game.

WEST—FOURTH PLAYER
(Third Play after Set)

West is the fourth player and in fourth set position. His first play must help his partner, who is on second set. His strategy depends upon whether or not his partner has drawn from the boneyard.

Partner Has Not Drawn from Boneyard

West must keep East, his partner, solvent and follow his partner's indicator. East's number should be considered his set and left alone. His first play is a key play for his team. Usually West can protect East, his partner, by keeping the game open and preventing the opponents from forcing his partner to draw from the deck. West should not be too concerned with his own hand. His first consideration is to help his partner (East) and hurt North.

North (setter) has set a double

1. South has played a singles off of your partner's domino.
   You must leave South's number alone. Play a double on South's number or play off of North's set as illustrated below.
   (a) Play off of North's (setter's) double.

This is a defensive play. It keeps the play open for your partner and helps to cut off setter's number.

A play on South's single putting up a new single number is a very bad play. It is a lead-back number and gives North an opportunity of converting it into his original number. This could send your partner (East) in for a lot of dominoes—a very dangerous play. Here is an illustration of what can happen.

Neither should you (West) make all of the ends the same number as North's original set.

This would be playing into North's hand. You should not risk this possibility unless you hold four of the number set, accounting for six—you would need to have a strong hand to do that or to determine that the set was a lighthouse. An exception may be made when you can make both ends 5's for a count of 3 points.

(b) Play double on South's number. This gives your partner two numbers to play on.

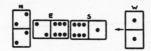

(c) If you cannot make one of the above plays, then play the domino that suits your hand best.

2. South has played off of his partner's double set.

(a) Play singles off of North's number (get around the double). Score, if possible, as with 2-0 or 2-5 in example below.

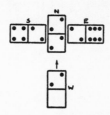

(b) Do not put up double on opponent's number unless you have kickers that will play off of the double, or you have a poor hand and want to get rid of dominoes to get hand over with—or you want to keep play open to do so, or

(c) Follow your partner's indicator. East, your partner, is on second set. If he did not score, his play indicates the number he likes and you must leave it alone. If you have a choice, put up his number.

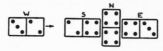

3. South has played a double on your partner's domino. This play has insured two numbers for North (setter) to play on.

(a) Score, if possible (as with 2-3 in example) or

(b) Play a number off of setter's double on which he cannot score (as a 2-1, in the example, if you hold the 1-3 in your hand).

(c) Cut down count, or

(d) Play number that suits your hand best.

North (setter) has set a singles domino

(a) If all of the dominoes on the table are singles and your opponent played off of your partner's number, cut off setter's (North) number, if possible.

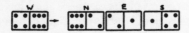

(b) If all of the dominoes on the table are singles and your opponent played off of his partner's number, leave your partner's number alone. Play off of your opponent's number or cross your partner's number with a double.

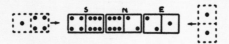

(c) If one of the dominoes on the table is a double, cut off the singles. This cuts off both of North's (setter's) numbers.

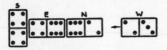

(d) If two of the dominoes on the table are doubles, score if possible; otherwise, cut down the count and put up the number that suits your hand.

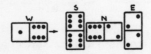

Partner Forced to Draw

When East, your partner, has been sent to the boneyard because he was unable to play on North's set, you must either open up the game or tighten it, as the circumstances dictate.

If your *partner has not gone in deep* you should provide your partner with three numbers to play on to prevent your opponents from sending him in again.

For example, North set the 3-3, and your partner was forced to draw. In his first or second draw he drew the 3-6. Now South played the 3-4 off of his partner's set, and it is your turn to play.

Play off of North's double if possible or play a double. 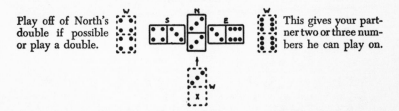 This gives your partner two or three numbers he can play on.

If East, your partner, *has drawn a lot of dominoes* you should play off of your opponent's set, build up the count, and tighten the game. In this way you may outscore your opponents and gain game control. *Avoid putting up doubles and leave your partner's number alone.*

PARTNER'S PET PEEVE

One of the most interesting hands in the game occurs when North sets a double and East goes to the boneyard for a load. The hand usually results in an exciting contest.

Since your team has most of the dominoes, the team on set will endeavor to keep both North and South solvent so that they may go out and get the count in your hands. Also, they will probably cut down the count and cut off the 5's to prevent your team from scoring heavily if possible.

Properly played, your hands can be made to produce some big scores for your team. *The secret is teamwork.* This means you must play to your partner's hand.

Many players do not know how to help East, their partner, when he has gone to the boneyard for a load. *West must play off of setter's double.* Some players refuse to play off of the setter's double because they are afraid that their opponents will take a big score. They hang on to their kicker or repeater for a possible score later. Consequently, costly misplays are made that help the opponents and prevent the partner from making the most of the dominoes in his hand. This is very frustrating and the pet peeve good players have against their partners.

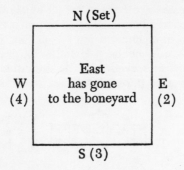

N (Set)

W (4)   East has gone to the boneyard   E (2)

S (3)

Here is an example of a botched play by a partner. North set the 3-3 and East went to the boneyard for six dominoes and drew the 3-6 which he played. He now has ten dominoes in his hand and no 3's. South played the 6-4 off of the 6. West held the 3-5, 3-4, 5-5, 4-0, and 6-1. He played the 4-0 off of the 4. North played the 0-2 off of the blank.

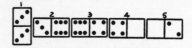

This leaves East only one number to play on, the 2. If he plays the 2-2, it puts up a double that perpetuates the 2. The 2-5, 2-4, and 2-1 are lead-back numbers to the 3. The only playable domino that will not lead back to a 3 is the 2-6. East is in trouble, and would have been in worse trouble if North had held and played the 0-3, making the 3's inviolate. The lack of teamwork on West's part will prove very costly because he, West, cannot control the game. It is fundamental that West must not play to his own hand. To gain control he must play to his partner's hand. If West had played, say, the 3-5, East would have had two or three plays, giving him an opportunity to score, set up his long suit, and indicate his strength to his partner. Let's see how it would have worked out if West had played the 3-5.

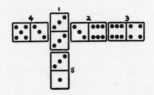

In the example each play-off of the 3-3 set eliminates one play-off of North's double and the number put up cannot be turned into a 3. This forces out new numbers on which East can play, score, or set up the numbers he can control. In the illustration North was forced to play off his set. East and West now know North has no 4's or 5's. East has most of the dominoes and by his next play, very likely off of the 1, will indicate to his partner which way he wants to go—to 4's, 5's, or score, as with the 1-6.

The Three Possibilities

If your team is off set and you or your partner has drawn a lot of dominoes from the boneyard, the first consideration is to gain game control, even though it may seem you are losing all. It may give your team an opportunity to go out, and the ideal situation would be for you or your partner, who has drawn all of the dominoes, to go out with lots of scoring. If your team succeeds in gaining game control, there is an opportunity to make a lot of points or, at least, to get rid of some large dominoes and reduce the count in your hands.

The next consideration is to buy your way out by scoring heavily. Scoring follows naturally when a player has a lot of dominoes in his hand.

The third consideration is to reduce the count and unload. When East has gone in on large numbers such as 6-6, the count in his hand is relatively small. East may have a lot of small dominoes and the situation may call for reducing the count on the table to keep the score down and at the same time getting rid of the large dominoes in the hand. In this way East may prevent the opponents from taking big scores and get the hand over with as cheaply as possible.

East Takes the Lead

When *you are East and have drawn* a lot of dominoes, you must decide which way you are going to go, for control or scores, and then, by your play, indicate to your partner your decision so that he can follow your lead.

If you have control of one or two numbers you have a chance to sabotage North by putting up the numbers you control. If you are trying for game control, this is what needs to be done.

1. Do not put up doubles unless it is one of the numbers you control.

2. Cut off new or lead-back numbers.
3. Put up the numbers you control.

If you do not have control of any numbers, then score and get rid of your large dominoes.

West Helps East

When *you are West and East, your partner, has drawn* a lot of dominoes, *he will try to get game control,* send the opponents to the boneyard, and put you on set, if possible. If he does not have control of any numbers, then *he will try to score.* For your partner to control the game or score heavily you must make the right plays when it comes your turn. This situation calls for teamwork *on your part.* Until your partner indicates otherwise you must assume he will attempt to gain game control. Here is the way to help your partner do it.

1. Play off of your opponent's double set (a must).
   This puts up numbers for your partner that do not lead back to the setter's number, gives your partner numbers to play on, and reduces the number of plays left on the opponent's set.
2. Do not put up doubles.
   A double perpetuates that number and opens up the game for the opponents.
3. Do not put up lead-back numbers to opponent's set.
   A playback enables the opponent to put up another of the number he set, which tightens the game for your partner and probably assures an out for the opponent.
4. Cut off lead-back numbers put up by your opponents.
   The knowledge gained in playing the hand will usually indicate the numbers that should be cut off.
5. Follow your partner's lead.
   Watch your partner's plays and put up the number indicated by him. This helps him get control.

If your partner decides, on his second or third play, that he is unable to gain control, and scores instead, then this is your cue to build up the count, score, if possible, and get rid of your big dominoes. In this case:

1. Play off of your opponent's double set (a must).
2. Build up the count.
   Since your partner has most of the dominoes, he has a lot of scoring combinations and a chance to make some big scores.
3. Score or get rid of big dominoes.

If your partner deliberately cuts down the count when the 6-6, 5-5, or 4-4 was set, you should follow his lead. Get rid of your large dominoes and reduce the count if possible.

Remember: For game control avoid playing doubles and cut off opponents' numbers. Cutting off a number means putting up another number. If you are West, you must watch your partner's (East) and your opponent's play carefully. Put up only *those numbers that back up your partner's hand*. This may be the same number he has put up or a number that has been played of which none or only one or two are left unplayed. In this way you avoid giving your opponent a brand-new number or one that leads back to his original number. To score heavily, build up the count.

This is the time and place to play bravely, tighten up the game, and snatch control away from your opponents.

Lesson No. 4—Second and Subsequent Rounds, Four-handed Game

All of the fundamental principles of play and favorable percentages will not help you if you do not have the right domino or, as some say, "the right ticket." Then, too, there are so many possible combinations in dominoes after four dominoes have been played that frequently plays or principles that are set forth appear to contradict each other and may seem confusing. Remember that very often it is necessary for the player to weigh one choice against another and then make what appears to be the best play or the one that offers the most favorable odds. Sometimes the choice will not work out well, even though your play was the best one. That is what makes the game intriguing. At first, while learning, do not worry too much about odds or favorable percentages. You will learn the favorable percentage plays and become more proficient with experience.

The plays advocated in the first round of four plays of each hand (when the player has a choice) are based upon favorable percentages. They are determined by algebraic calculations and the various odds are given in the sections where they are applicable. In the second and subsequent rounds of each hand there are so many possible combinations that it is practically impossible to predetermine the odds on each possible play, and any such figures would be valueless in actual play. When the favorable or unfavorable chances are important in making a choice, the practical thing to do is to determine the chances on that particular play. This is done by simple arithmetic and is explained in Part 6, "Making Your Choice of Plays."

POSITION IS THE THING

The basic strategy of each player in the second and subsequent rounds of each hand depends upon his playing position and the dominoes that have been played. The dominoes played tell a story, and you should have learned something from what has been played and who has played it. The basic fundamentals of play in the second and subsequent rounds of a four-handed game are explained in this chapter in the order of play, thus:

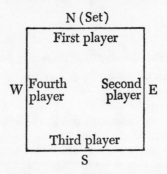

N (Set)

First player

W   Fourth player   Second player   E

Third player

S

NORTH—PLAYER ON SET

The player on original set is in the first position to go out. This is a preferred position and gives the team a real advantage. The setter should do everything to maintain that position.

Player on Set Must Keep Solvent

The player on set has the prime responsibility of keeping himself in a position of being able to play and go out. This is important. He must establish the suit (number) he has most of and remain solvent if possible.

There are times when one has a choice between taking a score or assure going out. The problem is whether to play the domino that gives a sure out or the domino that scores but does not assure another play. In general, the player on set should not speculate and score except under favorable or advantageous circumstances as follows:

1. You can score 5 or more points.
2. You can get off a possible "skunk."
3. You can assure winning the game.
4. The opponent on your left has drawn from the boneyard and your partner is on second set.
5. The domino in your hand is a singles and both numbers are open (provided several have been played and chances of them being cut off are remote).

When to Play Off of Your Own Set

When three plays have been made on your double set it is advisable to play on the fourth side before your opponents cut off the number.

Illustration: You set the 4-4 and three plays have been made on your set, leaving only the fourth side open.

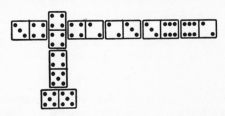

It is your turn to play. You hold the 4-6. You can also play on the 2. If you don't play on the fourth side of your double set someone else will very probably play on it and you may never get rid of your 4-6. Say you elect to hold the 4-6 and play on the 2 instead. The next player plays on the 4-4, cutting off the 4's. Now if your partner should put up a 6, which is a new or lead-back number, your opponent will surely cut it off. On the other hand, if you played the 4-6, there are four numbers on which you can play and your partner will realize you need numbers and will cross one of the numbers, if possible, thus setting up a new double for you. Then, too, your opponents must put up doubles or put up new numbers which you can play on.

Force Opponent on Left to Draw

By forcing your opponent to your left to draw, you force him off second set position and put your partner on second set. This makes South, your partner, vice-president. It gives your team two chances to go out, and you may catch your opponents with a large count in their hands.

Illustration: You set the 0-0. It is your turn to play and you hold the 2-0.

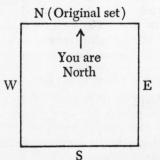

This play could send your opponent to the boneyard for a load and place your partner on second set. The next play must bring up a new number. If your partner can cross it, your team could be in an excellent position to go out and score a lot of points.

Get Rid of Doubles

At the first opportunity you must get rid of doubles, even at risk of opponent scoring. This disposes of a domino that may be difficult to play later and it sets up that number.

Play Off of Singles

To insure going out, plays should be made on singles. Hold dominoes that will play on spinners (doubles) unless you are "wired" to go out. Generally it is good practice to pass up two or three points and make sure of going out.

Protect Numbers in Your Hand

When you have several dominoes with the same number, protect that number by getting up two or more to assure your subsequent plays.

When You Are Forced Off Set

When you have gone off original set, your strategy depends upon who has gone on set.

If East, your opponent to your left, has gone on set, force him to draw, if possible, thus putting your partner on set. It is your (North's) responsibility to force East off set, even if you are cutting your partner's throat, because South, your partner, can't be on set until East is forced to draw.

If South, your partner, is on set, open up the game by playing doubles and putting up as many numbers as possible.

If West, your opponent to your right, has gone on set, tighten up the game and support your partner to get game control if possible.

EAST—SECOND PLAYER
(On Original Second Set)

This player is on original second set and should endeavor to stay solvent unless he was forced to draw on his first play so that he may go out if the player on set goes off set.

Establish Own Numbers

Play doubles on your own number or partner's numbers. This provides additional plays.

When you put up numbers, play the numbers that you have most of in your hand. The more dominoes with a particular number you have, the better chance there is of that number holding up and the less chance of your opponent (setter) and his partner having that number.

Cut Off Opponent's Set

The domino that was set is the opponent's primary number and, consequently, it is your first target. If it is a double, the strategy is to attack and play on the setter's double, and if a singles, to cut off both numbers.

Avoid Playing Doubles on Setter's Numbers

Generally you should avoid playing a double on the setter's numbers because by doing so you perpetuate that number for him.

As a general rule, it is a good practice to cut off numbers put up by the setter. This blocks his play and prevents him from establishing his numbers.

Cut Off Singles Played by Setter

Since you cannot cut off the numbers of the opponent to your left and the opponent to your right, you must make a choice between them. Generally it is better to cut off the numbers played by the setter and play to your own hand even though the setter is probably discarding a domino and holding one he can play on the double he set. Your play may not hurt his hand and may actually help him if the number he played is cut off. However, this is a chance you take when you make this play.

From this position it is practically impossible for you to send the player to your right to the boneyard. At best all you can hope to do is to cut off a number which he may need and prevent his partner from crossing it with a double or scoring.

Get Rid of Doubles

After the first or second round, get rid of doubles. This disposes of a domino that may be difficult to play later. You may help your opponent, but you are also helping your partner and yourself.

Forced to Draw

When you are forced to draw, you automatically go off second set and your opponents are now both on set and on second set.

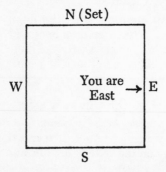

When you are forced to draw, your strategy is to tighten the game and build up the count. This may force South, your opponent to your left, to the boneyard and put your partner on second set. Remember, you have a partner to help you. If your opponent scores, your partner will probably score, too, and when your turn comes you may be able to score some nice points. This is the time to trust your partner and for your partner to trust you. You should depend on your partner to score and send North, the player on set, to the boneyard. If you have drawn a lot of dominoes, your partner will help you get game control if possible. This is fairly easy to do, as you have practically all of the dominoes.

If North goes off set, force South to draw, if possible, thus putting West, your partner, on set.

If West, your partner, should go on set, then your strategy changes. In this event you should open up the game by playing doubles and putting up as many numbers as possible to assure his going out.

Partner Forced to Draw

When your partner is forced to draw, you must give him numbers he can play on and which will prevent your opponents from sending him in again. The way to do this is to play a double on his number or the number put up by your opponent to your right, or a new single number that cannot be made the same as the number he was sent in on. For example:

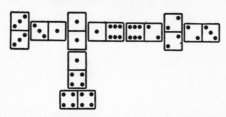

West was forced to draw and drew the 4-4. North played the 3-3. It is your turn to play. Your partner cannot play on the 1, 2, 3, or 4. He needs 6's, 5's, and blanks. If you put up blanks or 5's they will surely be cut off and turned into 1, 2, 3, or 4. The best number to put up is a 6. In the example 4-6 would be an excellent play, as it cannot be turned into a 1, 2, or 4.

When your partner's turn comes to play again, watch his play carefully. If he tightens the game, help him get game control and follow his lead on the numbers he pushes.

SOUTH—THIRD PLAYER
(Partner of Player on Set)

It is more important to make the proper play to insure your partner's position by keeping the play open for him so that he may go out than it is for you to score.

Put up Doubles

Generally the best way to help your partner on set and protect his hand is to put up doubles. The more doubles played, the more certain he is of scoring and going out.

If your partner sets a singles domino (two numbers), you must assume he holds one or more of each in his hand and you must cross either one with a double if possible. If you are unable to cross your partner's number, then cross the opponent's number if you can.

Give Your Partner Numbers

It is your responsibility to help your partner. The way to do this is to give him new numbers or play another of a new number to prevent that number from being cut off. By adding numbers you give your partner valuable help and increase the odds of his being able to play. If you can score, too, so much the better.

There is an old maxim, "Once off your partner's double." Like any other rule, it has its exceptions and depends upon the situation. On the first time around this is a good rule, but not necessarily on subsequent plays. If you took a score on the first round of the hand and no plays have been made off of your partner's double set, one play should be made off of his double, but if the game has been opened, it is well to leave his double alone.

Do Not Cut Off Partner's Numbers

The most frequent error made by the setter's partner is cutting off his partner's numbers. Usually when your partner puts up a number it means he wants that number to follow up his play and is informing you he wants that particular number. Of course there are circumstances where it is necessary to play on your partner's number. If it cannot be avoided, give him back his number as soon as you can.

As a general rule, do not cover your partner's domino when you have a choice.

Exceptions:

1. The opponent to your right has drawn a large number of dominoes and you can assure going out in the event your partner gets into trouble.
2. To assure going out or to prevent a "skunk."
3. When you are able to score and are fairly sure the next player cannot follow with a score, as with the 5-5, or you feel that your play and score will assist your partner.
4. When you are able to help your partner by getting up numbers for him to play on and there is no indication from your hand

or the plays made that your partner needs that particular number.

If you must make a choice, play a double or put up a new number, or cut off the opponent's number in preference to cutting off your partner's number. Remember, your opponents are trying to establish numbers that suit their hands.

Avoid Cutting Off Opponent's Number

Do not attempt to send the opponent to your right to the bone-yard for dominoes. This tightens up the game and forces your partner to play valuable dominoes he may need later, or may even force him off set. If it can be avoided, do not cut off numbers including those put up by your opponents.

If you must cut off a number and have a choice, cut off a number your partner passed up on a previous play.

Forced to Draw

When you are forced to the boneyard and draw a playable domino you must keep numbers open, not cut them off. It now becomes doubly important for your partner to go out and you must give him all the help you can.

Partner Forced Off Set

When your partner is forced off set, your strategy depends on which player is on set.

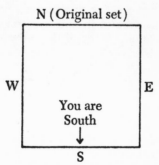

If *East is on set* your strategy is to build up the count and tighten the game to enable North to put you on set if possible. Forget about scoring. Your strategy and your partner's is to get East off the set. Remember, you have a partner to help you get on set.

If you have scoring dominoes in your hand, you can depend upon your partner having picked up some scoring dominoes in his drawing—depending on the numbers he was sent in on—if 6's he has small dominoes in his hand. So you should score if you hold good scoring dominoes and depend upon your partner scoring, too.

Basically, you must depend upon your partner to send East, the player on set, to the boneyard if possible. If North has drawn a lot of dominoes, he will try to get you on set. If this should happen, then of course you should do everything possible to keep solvent and go out.

If you are on set you must keep solvent and go out if possible.

If West is on set, force him to draw if possible, putting North, your partner, back on set.

WEST—FOURTH PLAYER
(Partner of Player on Original Second Set)

This player's prime objective is to force the player on set to go off set and, second, to prevent his partner on second set from being sent to the boneyard.

The player to his left (North) is the one he wants to send to the boneyard. At every opportunity he should cut off the setter's numbers or those the setter may need. The setter is the man this player wants to get.

Cover Opponent's Set

The domino that was set is this player's primary target. If a double was set, play around it, and if a singles was set, follow your partner's indication. If one of the setter's numbers is open, it should be cut off if possible.

Cut Off Numbers

The primary strategy of this player is to tighten the game for the one on set. The way to do this is to cut off single numbers and doubles. The player in this position may cut off numbers *without regard to which player put them up,* if by doing so he can force the setter off set.

New numbers put up by the setter's partner should be cut off, particularly when the setter is in a playing position to go out.

Avoid Putting up New Numbers

Frequently new numbers will enable the team on set to score or go out. Tighten the game by reducing the open numbers or get rid of a double instead. In this way you do not change the numbers that are open and this will force your opponent to put up new numbers that your partner can play on. If you put up new numbers, you may give your opponent many plays that will help him go out and combinations to score with, or he may be able to tighten the game and send your partner to the boneyard. However, if your partner is in trouble, give him a number that will enable him to play.

Put up Partner's Numbers

Your partner is on second set and wants to establish his numbers. As a general rule, do not cut off your partner's numbers, instead, put them up. Play doubles on his numbers or put up another of that number to prevent it being cut off. If your partner indicates he likes a number by pushing it, give him more of that number, as it probably suits his hand and tightens the game for the opponents.

Opponent Forced Off Set

When you succeed in forcing North, your opponent, off set and your partner goes on set, your strategy changes. Now your objective is to get your partner out, thus you play doubles or give your partner numbers and open up the game.

Forced to Draw

When you are forced to draw and North is still on set, tighten the game by cutting off your opponents' numbers to force North off set if possible, thus putting your partner on set.

Partner Forced to Draw

When your partner is forced to draw, your opponents are both on set and on second set.

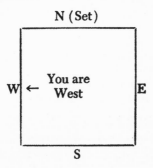

Your strategy is to build up the count and tighten the game. This may force North, your opponent to your left, to the boneyard, and may help your partner get game control. Remember, you have a partner to help you. If you succeed in forcing both North and South to the boneyard, then you go on set. You must depend upon your partner to send South to the boneyard if possible. If he has drawn a lot of dominoes, he may get game control, score a lot of points, and get you out.

This is the time to get game control. You must cut off opponents' numbers and avoid putting up doubles or new numbers for your opponents to play on.

Lesson No. 5—Basic Strategy, Two-handed Game

The basic strategy in the two-handed Five-up game is different from that in the four-handed partnership game. In the two-handed game the principal emphasis is on defense and protecting your hand. The four-handed and the three-handed games are more open and the accent is on aggressive plays.

In the four-handed game twenty dominoes are in the four players' hands with only eight remaining in the deck. Consequently, more dominoes are played and more numbers will come up than in the two-handed game. If an opponent scores, the chances are that your partner will have some kickers and will score, too. In the two-handed game the two players hold only ten dominoes with eighteen in the deck. Fewer dominoes and less numbers are played. The odds are greater in the two-handed game of the players being forced to the boneyard with the possibility of drawing many dominoes before finding the needed number.

In the two-handed game you have no partner to worry about and you can take unfavorable chances. Sometimes a long risk will pay off handsomely. However, as the unfavorable chances are greater in two-handed than in four-handed games, usually it is better to base your plays on favorable percentage. They work out best in the long run.

SETTER—OPENING PLAY

The main objective of the set is to *establish the number you have most of* to assure future plays. Scoring is secondary and you should resist the temptation to score unless it is the proper set. Here is a guide based on favorable percentage.

1. Set a double provided you have another *matching* domino.

Exceptions:

    (a) A 5-5 "lighthouse" is a good set if you hold some *blanks*.
    (b) A "lighthouse" is a good set if you hold *six* different numbers.
    (c) Set a "lighthouse" if you have no singles domino that gives you a play on *both ends*.

2. Do not set the double when you hold *five* of that suit.
3. Set a singles domino that gives you a chance to play on *either* end.
4. Set the singles domino of your longest suit.

OPPONENT—FIRST PLAY

When your opponent is on set, your first objective should be to keep the game as open as possible for yourself in order to avoid going to the boneyard. To accomplish this you have to *establish the numbers you have most of* and cut off your opponent's numbers, if possible. This means making the right play in preference to scoring. Here is a guide based on favorable percentage:

1. Play a double if you have one that is playable.
2. Play a singles domino that will *get up two numbers* you can play on, if possible. This will assure your next play.
3. Do not cut yourself off, but play a domino that will leave you at least one play if possible.

CHOICE OF PLAYS

When you have a choice of plays, follow the "four basic principles" explained in Part 3—"How to Plan Your Strategy." They are based on favorable percentage. The player who *consistently* makes the plays with the percentage or odds in his favor will win more times than he loses. This is how they apply to the two-handed game.

1. Look forward to the next play.
    Score if you can, but protect your hand by making each move so you can follow with another play. Generally, pass up a score if necessary to keep the play open for yourself, to insure

going out on the hand or to send your opponent to the bone-yard when you have a sure out.

(a) Play doubles at first opportunity.

(b) Play a domino that gives you a play on either end.

(c) Play off single number in preference to double.

(d) Hold kickers and repeaters.

(e) Avoid plays that give your opponent a lead-back number.

(f) Reduce opponent's chances to score.

(g) If you cannot score, reduce the count on the table unless you hold good scoring dominoes or it is to your advantage to build up the count.

2. Do not force opponent to draw unless you can go out or your chances of going out are good.

A large number of dominoes in your opponent's hand, skill-fully played, can add up to a lot of points.

3. Do not tighten game when you have no further play.

It is very dangerous to cut off all numbers except one when you have no number to play on it. If possible, give yourself two numbers to play on.

Say your opponent set the 4-4 and he has now played the 3-6. The only playable domino in your hand is the 6-4, and you have no other 4 or 6.

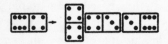

In case you have to draw, your chances of drawing a playable number will be much more favorable.

3. When your opponent is in trouble, cut off the numbers he puts up.

When a player plays off of a double without scoring, generally he is in trouble because fundamentally one will play off of a singles in preference to a double. Generally, the best play is to cut off the number put up by the opponent.

4. Control the game when you are forced to draw a large number of dominoes.

When you draw a large number of dominoes from the bone-yard with a big count, you can tell fairly well which dominoes your opponent has left. You must block your opponent and force him to draw from the boneyard or you should build up the count and score to offset the points left in your hand, or both, if possible.

When your opponent is down to his last domino he can have only two numbers and only one if the domino is a double. By observing closely the numbers your opponent could not play on and the possible plays not made, you can see what number he needs to go out. Frequently this is the last number put up, particularly if the opponent plays off of a double.

LESSON NO. 6—BASIC STRATEGY, THREE-HANDED GAME (IGORROTE)

Three persons may play the Five-up game with twenty-eight dominoes. The game is 61 points. Each player draws five dominoes. This leaves thirteen in the boneyard.

The game is played in the same way as a two-handed game except that each player scores independently. The game is more erratic than in a two-handed game, where you have only one player to play against. Here you have two players to contend with. In the four-handed game you have a partner to help you. In the three-handed game each player tries to defeat the other two in a free-for-all. Hence the nickname "Igorrote" after the tribe of head hunters, the "Igorrotes."

A very interesting variation of the "Igorrote" game, called "Cut-throat," is described in the Official Rules under "Optional Rules and Penalties."

SCORING

Points are scored on the plays in exactly the same way as in two- and four-handed games. The player who goes out on the hand receives the points the other two players have in their hands. Between the two players with dominoes left in their hands, the one with the least *points* receives the difference between the points in his hand and the points in the other player's hand.

The game is completed when one of the players reaches 61 points or more. If two or three players all have 61 points or more, the player with the highest score wins. In the case of a tie between the players ahead, three additional hands are played to give each player an opportunity to set. In a tie game, it is possible for the player who is behind to win the game.

The winner of the game receives from each of the other two players the difference between his score and their score (plus agreed points, if any, from each for winning the game). The player with the *next highest* score receives the difference between his score and the other player's score, but nothing is added for going out. If "skunks" are agreed upon, the agreed penalty is applied by the player who won the game only against the player(s) who was skunked.

Scoring is the most important strategy. The points scored on a play or for going out are worth twice as much in a three-handed game as they are in a two- or four-handed game because the points count against the other two players.

SETTER—OPENING PLAY

You should set the domino that will give you the most plays. Score if possible. Here is a general guide based on favorable odds.

1. Set double, even if it is a "lighthouse" (including 5-5).
2. Set a singles that gives you a play on either end.

GENERAL STRATEGY

1. Protect your set position. Put up doubles or numbers to assure an out.
2. Score; very few situations justify passing up a score.
3. Force opponents to draw. Tighten game. Force out new numbers.
4. Get rid of doubles at first opportunity.
5. Reduce count if you can't score.
6. Avoid plays that give your opponents a lead-back number.
7. Play against leader.

When one player gets far ahead on points, you and the other player should work together to prevent the leader from going out, if possible. If necessary, pass up a score. Only by cooperating with the other player do either of you have an opportunity of overcoming the leader. To play alone is to go down in defeat.

PART 8

Official Rules for Five-up Game

OFFICIAL RULES FOR FIVE-UP DOMINO GAME

Adopted by the

INTERNATIONAL DOMINO ASSOCIATION

The official rules of play for the Five-up domino game, hereinafter set forth, have been adopted by the International Domino Association (I.D.A.). These rules are followed by players, groups, all major tournaments, and at clubs where the game is played.

Many players have long recognized the need for a standard set of rules of play. Uniform rules avoid conflicts and misunderstandings, add to the players' enjoyment, and promote a widespread interest in this fascinating game. To fill this need the author reviewed the rules adopted by many clubs and those followed by players generally and from these compiled a set of rules that were submitted to a group of experienced players for consideration. The members of this advisory group have participated in many tournaments or have acted as chairmen of the domino committees of their own clubs and are well qualified to pass judgment on proper rules of play. This advisory committee agreed upon rules of play for the Five-up game of dominoes. Some important changes in the original rules have since been made and they are incorporated in the current rules.

Clubs, tournaments, players, or groups may now establish recognized and uniform rules of play by adopting the I.D.A. rules.

The International Domino Association is a nonprofit association organized to promote the great game of dominoes, standardize the rules, sanction charitable tournaments, and award master points.

I.D.A. conducts tournaments for its members and publishes information on domino activities. Anyone of good character may join the Association.

For information regarding membership, tournaments, or master points write to:

International Domino Association
465 California Street, Room 1500
San Francisco, California 94104

RULES OF PLAY

Dominoes

The game is played with the standard set of 28 dominoes. Each domino has two sections. Spots on each section represent a number or a blank, from six down through blank. The domino set is arranged in such a way that 21 pieces have two different numbers or a blank, as 6-1 or 5-0, and seven pieces have two of the same number or blank, as 6-6 or 0-0.

Players

1. Two, three, or four may play.
2. The two- and three-handed games are played as singles.
3. The four-handed game is played as doubles and the players pair off as partners. Partners may be determined by draw or mutual consent; if by draw, the two highs play the two lows.

Basic Rules

1. Basic playing procedure and rules are the same in two-, three-, and four-handed games, except as indicated under each rule.
2. These rules apply unless changed by agreement before commencement of play.
3. Rules and penalties on exposed dominoes, misplays, underdrawing, overdrawing, reneging, errors in scoring and pegging, and giving information are covered under *Irregularities*.
4. There are no scores, penalties, or rules other than those specifically stated in this set of rules, or those agreed upon before commencement of play.
5. Specific rules for tournaments are covered under *Tournament Rules*.
6. The player claiming a penalty, or the application of a rule to a particular play, is responsible for pointing out the rule that applies.

Game

1. The game is 61 points.
2. The team that reaches 61 points or more at the finish of any

hand wins the game. If both teams reach 61 points or more, the team that is ahead wins.

3. The last hand must be played out.

4. The team that wins receives the difference between the scores made by the two teams. As an example: if Team A made 67 points and Team B made 49 points, Team A would win by 18 points. If the game is played for any optional additional points, such as for winning or for a skunk, they are added to the points won.

Partners and Set

1. All dominoes are placed face down on the table and mixed thoroughly by any player.

2. Each player draws one domino and shows it to the other players to determine who shall be partners and who sets first. If two players both draw the same valued dominoes, then the one with the highest end prevails, i.e., 6-4 is higher than 5-5.

3. The player who draws the highest domino is *on set*. He has the choice of seats, and plays first.

4. The set rotates after each hand to the left (clockwise).

Original Draw

1. After the set is determined, all dominoes are placed face down and mixed thoroughly by the player to the right of the setter.

2. The setter draws any five dominoes. The other players, to his left, each in turn (clockwise), draw five dominoes.

3. The five dominoes drawn become the player's hand and cannot be returned to the deck.

Boneyard

1. The dominoes left in the deck, after all the players have drawn their hands, remain face down and become the boneyard. The boneyard is placed to the right of the player on set for further use as provided by the rules. If the dominoes are moved toward a player to facilitate drawing, it is the responsibility of the setter to return the remaining dominoes to his right.

2. The dominoes in the boneyard may not be exposed during play. If any are exposed, they must be shown to all players immediately and the boneyard re-mixed.

The Play

1. Each player, in his turn, plays one domino.
2. The player *on set* plays first. He may play any domino in his hand.
3. The play rotates to the left (clockwise).
4. If a player has a playable domino in his hand, he must play from his hand. He may not pass or draw from the boneyard. A playable domino is any domino in the player's hand with a number matching an open end of the layout on the table.
5. A doubles domino must be played across the matching number.
6. A singles domino may be played off the end of another matching singles, or off of both sides and both ends of any double. The first and second domino played on the double must be played off of the sides of the double (across).
7. Plays on a singles may be made only once, off of each end.
8. A domino is considered played when the player has taken his hand off of it.
9. The dominoes in each player's hand may not be exposed to the other players, but at all times must be kept on the table in full view of the other players.

Setting

1. Any domino may be set.
2. The domino that is set should be pointed by the setter in a uniform direction, thus indicating the player on set. A double should be set horizontal to the setter. A single should be set vertical to the setter, with the highest number toward him.

Scoring Plays

1. If the open ends of the dominoes on the table total five or a multiple of five, then the team that makes the combination shall receive one point for each five count on the table. If the count is not a multiple of five, there is no score.
2. All spots on a double are counted *only* when it is an end.

Inability to Play

1. If a player has no domino that enables him to play to the open ends of the dominoes on the table, he shall draw from the

boneyard until he secures a domino that will play. The dominoes drawn become part of his hand.

(a) In a three- or four-handed game, all of the dominoes in the boneyard, with the exception of one, may be drawn.

(b) In a two-handed game, all of the dominoes in the boneyard, with the exception of two, may be drawn.

2. If a player is unable to play or draw, he passes until he can play in his turn.

Completion of Hand

1. When any one of the players succeeds in playing all of his dominoes, the hand is completed.

2. At the end of the hand, the dominoes remaining in each player's hand must be turned face up on the table and shown to all of the players.

Count Remaining in Hands

The player or team who has *dominoed* or *gone out* shall add all the spots upon the dominoes remaining in the opponents' hands and receive one point for each count of five, and one more if the count remaining amounted to three or four. Remainders of one and two are disregarded.

(a) In a four-handed game the team that goes out receives the points for the combined count in their opponents' hands. The count in the hand of the partner of the player who goes out is disregarded.

(b) In a three-handed game the player who goes out receives the points in each of the other two players' hands. Each is counted separately. Between the two remaining players, the one with the lowest number of points receives the difference between the points in his hand and the points in the other player's hand.

(c) In a two-handed game, the player who goes out receives the points in his opponent's hand.

Blocked Hand

If all but one of the dominoes have been drawn from the boneyard (two in a two-handed game), and the players each have one or more dominoes, but are still unable to play any one of them, the hand is *blocked.* All of the players turn their dominoes face up, and count the spots on the dominoes in their hands.

(a) In a four-handed game, the team with the lowest combined count receives all the points in the opponents' hands. If the combined count remaining in the two teams' hands is the same, there is no score.

As an example: A and B's combined count is 16, and C and D's is 39, then A and B's team receives the value of 39, or 8 points. A and B's count is 21, and C and D's count is 20, then C and D's team receives the value of 21, or 4 points.

(b) In a three-handed game, only the player with the lowest count receives the points in the other player's hand. He receives the difference between the points in his hand and the points in each of the other two player's hands. In the event the low count is tied, there is no score.

(c) In a two-handed game, the player with the lowest count receives all the points in his opponent's hand. If the count is tied, there is no score.

Pegging Points Scored

1. The points scored should be pegged on a scoreboard. Each hole represents one point.

2. When a score is made it must be claimed before the next play is completed. A score not claimed, before the next player has played, is passed and may not be pegged, but the next player can take a score if he plays a scoring domino.

3. A score cannot be taken on the last play of the hand if the score is claimed after the dominoes in the layout on the table have been moved.

Start of New Hand

After the first hand, the set rotates to the left (clockwise). The player to the right of the one on set mixes the dominoes for the new setter. The play continues as in the previous hand.

Tie Game

If the game ends in a tie, two additional hands shall be played to determine the winner of two-handed and four-handed games, and three additional hands shall be played to determine the winner of three-handed games. In a three-handed game, if two players are tied for game, the third player also plays in the playoff.

Start of New Game

1. In a four-handed game, the losers of the game set first in the next game, and either partner may set, as decided before drawing. If players change partners, players draw for set and seat.

2. In a two-handed game, the loser sets first.

3. In a three-handed game, the player with the lowest score in the preceding game sets first.

IRREGULARITIES—RULES AND PENALTIES

Exposed Dominoes

Defined: A domino is considered exposed when one end of the domino is identified by any other player.

Player's hand:

1. If a player exposes a domino during the draw of his hand, or in his hand after the draw, the domino must be turned face up and played at the first opportunity. If more than one domino is exposed, the opponents may demand which domino shall be played, but may not direct where it shall be played if it plays in more than one position.

2. If a domino in a player's hand is deliberately exposed by any other player, the domino shall be returned to the player's hand and the opponents of the player who exposed the domino shall receive *three* points.

3. In a four-handed game, if the player who is on set position exposes the last domino in his hand before his partner's play, he may not go out on the hand and he may not draw from the boneyard.

Making the play:

1. A domino is played when it is placed in a playable position and the player has removed his hand from it. Until the player removes his hand, the domino may be placed wherever it plays. Once a domino is exposed, it may not be returned to the player's hand. If the domino is not playable, it must be turned face up on the table and played at the first opportunity.

2. If a player commences to play a domino and then attempts to return it to his hand, either opponent may identify one end of the domino and demand that it be played at the first opportunity. The opponent may not direct where it shall be played if it plays in more than one position. If the domino is not called, it may be returned to the player's hand.

3. If an opponent elects to call a domino which he claimed was exposed by the player and does not correctly identify one end of the domino, *three* points shall be awarded to the player's team, and the player need not play the domino at the first opportunity. Incorrect identification may be proved, at the player's option, by either (a) immediately turning the domino face up, or (b) separating it from the other dominoes in the player's hand and turning it face up when played or at the end of the hand.

4. If it is proved that a player who has exposed a domino has not acknowledged its correct identification, the opponents shall receive 9 points.

Boneyard:

1. If, while drawing, a player exposes a domino in the boneyard, he must keep it, turn it face up, and play it at the first opportunity.

2. If a domino in the boneyard is exposed other than by a player while drawing, it must be shown to all of the players, returned to the boneyard face down, and mixed thoroughly with the other dominoes.

3. The last domino in the boneyard (or the last two in a two-handed game) may not be looked at by any player. If a player looks at the last domino(es), the domino must be turned face up and the opponents shall receive *three* points.

Misplays

1. If a player misplays a domino, for instance a 6 end on a 5 end, and the domino is playable elsewhere, either opponent may demand that it be played correctly.

2. If a player attempts to play a domino that is not playable anywhere, it must be returned to the player's hand, left face up, and played at the first opportunity.

3. If a misplay is made and not discovered until after the next player has played, the misplay shall stand and the play must continue as if no misplay was made. If the next player has drawn

from the boneyard and looked at a domino, he must continue drawing until he can play or is forced to pass.

4. If a player plays out of turn, the domino played is considered an exposed domino. It must be returned to the player's hand, left face up, and played at the first opportunity. If the next player has also played out of turn, both plays stand, and the play must continue as if no misplay had been made. The player skipped loses his overlooked play.

Underdrawing

If a player draws less than five dominoes to his original hand he must complete his draw when his underdraw is discovered. If his underdraw is discovered when no more dominoes may be drawn from the boneyard, the player may not go out. This is the only penalty.

Overdrawing

Draw of hands: If a player draws more than five dominoes to his original hand, he must keep all he has looked at. He may not score for as many plays following discovery of the overdraw as the number of dominoes he drew exceeding five. This is the only penalty.

Drawing from boneyard:

1. If a player overlooks a playable domino in his hand and draws from the boneyard, he must keep all dominoes drawn. Upon discovering his overdraw, he must immediately announce it, and the opponents shall receive *three* points. He may not score during the remainder of his hand, but his partner may score.

If the player who overdraws announces it before the hand is completed, but after he has scored subsequent to his overdraw, the opponents shall receive *six* points. He may not score during the remainder of his hand, but his partner may score.

If the player who overdraws fails to announce it before the hand is completed, the opponents shall receive *nine* points.

In any event, the player's team shall still receive the count in the opponents' hands if the player's team goes out.

2. If a player draws the last domino in the boneyard (last two in a two-handed game) and looks at it, he has overdrawn. The domino may not be played and must be turned face up; the op-

ponents shall receive *three* points and the player may not score for the remainder of the hand.

Reneging

A player may not pass if he has a playable domino in his hand, or where more than one domino (two in a two-handed game) remain in the boneyard. If a player passes, and the next player completes his play, the pass is a renege. Upon discovery of the renege, the player must immediately announce it, and the opponents shall receive *three* points, which is the only penalty. If the next player also reneges, without calling the previous player's renege, the penalty against the previous player is passed.

Errors in Scoring and Pegging

1. If a score is not claimed before the next player has played, it may not be pegged.
2. If an error or oversight in pegging a score is not claimed before the next player has played, the error or oversight must stand.
3. If a score is taken on a miscount and the error is not discovered until after the next player has played, the score taken on the miscount stands.

Penalty Points

Penalty points for irregularities shall be paid by the advancing of the score and not by setting back the penalized team.

Giving Information

1. A player may not suggest a play or impart information to his partner by word or deed, except:
   (a) To call the total count on the table before or after the partner's play;
   (b) To claim a score made by his partner before the next play is completed;
   (c) To name open numbers in the layout on the table when the partner is about to draw from boneyard.

If a play is suggested or information is conveyed by the partner, the team may not count a score on the suggested play.

2. If the player whose turn it is to play accepts an incorrect count of the dominoes on the table as correct, his play must remain. If the error is discovered before the next play, his play must be counted correctly to score.

3. The last domino must be played exactly as other plays. Giving information on the last play, as on all other plays, is prohibited.

INTERPRETATION OF RULES

If the interpretation of a rule or the application of a penalty by an opponent is not accepted as correct by the player against whom it is levied, the following shall apply:

1. In a four-handed game, the player against whom the rule is applied should state the facts and abide by a decision reached by his partner and the partner of the opponent who applied the rule to the play.

2. In a three-handed game the player against whom the rule is applied should state the facts and abide by a decision reached by the other two players.

3. If the disagreement cannot be resolved by the players in tournament play, the official judge, whose decision shall be final, should be consulted for a ruling on any dispute or infraction of the rules. When there is no official judge, the players shall select an arbitrator from the domino committee, a kibitzer, or another domino player whose decision shall be final.

OPTIONAL RULES, SCORES, AND PENALTIES

There are several optional rules, scores, and penalties that some domino players like to apply to the game. The ones more widely used are given here for players who may wish to use them by *agreement before commencement of play.* In tournament games only the standard rules apply.

Ten Points for Winning Game

Most players like to play for points and game. The usual practice is to give the winner 10 points for winning the game. The value of the game is usually fixed at ten times the value of 1 point.

This makes it easy to keep track of the total points won or lost by each player. This 10-point rule applies when the players agree to "play for points and game" unless a different number is stipulated. In a three-handed game, only the winner receives the agreed game bonus points for winning the game.

Double for Skunks

It may be decided that if one team scores 61 points or more before the other team has scored 31 points, this shall be considered a skunk.

The penalty for a skunk game is double the total of the points won or lost, including the points for game. This rule applies when the players agree to play "skunks" unless a different penalty is stipulated.

In a three-handed game only the winner receives the agreed penalty.

Two Points for Going Out

Some players give the team or player who dominoes on the hand two points for going out. This has the effect of speeding up the game and putting a premium on going out. This rule may be applied to two-, three-, or four-handed games.

Ten Points for Five Doubles

Five doubles in one player's hand in the original draw of five dominoes occurs very infrequently (one time out of 4,680). Under the rules the hand is treated the same as any other. Some players like to make such a hand a windfall rather than a disaster and automatically give the player who drew the hand of five doubles 10 points. When this rule is applied, the five doubles must be shown before commencement of play and the hand is considered completed. The set rotates and the players draw new hands in the usual manner.

Set in Succeeding Games

It may be decided that the losers of each game played shall set first in the next game, and that either partner may set as decided before drawing.

PART 9

Rules for Other Domino Games

RULES FOR OTHER DOMINO GAMES

There are many games played with dominoes throughout the world. Since these games and the variations are so numerous, the rules given here are limited to the most popular games currently played with the standard set of European dominoes, starting with the 6-6. Both the names and rules of some of these games vary in different parts of the country and among players. The most common method of play is the one given here. Where the name is not well established, the most descriptive is used.

There are two types of games played with European dominoes. They include "matching" games and "card" games played with dominoes.

All of the "matching" games are played by placing a domino adjacent to one already on the table. The domino must match that upon which it is playable. The games vary according to the rule governing the play when a player has no playable domino, and also the scoring in the course of play. In the "block" game he loses his turn. In the "draw" games he draws from the boneyard until he gets one that can play. In the "block" games there is no scoring during the course of play. In the "scoring" games there are both drawing from the boneyard and scoring during play.

Many "card" games have been adopted to play with dominoes. Some were particularly popular in sections of the United States where playing cards were considered immoral. Most of these domino games are inferior to the original card games and have largely disappeared as the old prejudice vanished. Only three still flourished: Forty-two, an adaptation of Auction Pitch; Bingo, based on bezique; and Rum, a poker game played with the 12-12 domino set with ninety-one pieces.

Most of the games played in this country use the standard set of twenty-eight dominoes, and each player draws either five or seven dominoes in the original hand.

SEVEN-TOED PETE (RACE HORSE)

SEVEN-DRAW SCORING GAME WITH REPEATER PLAYS

This is a fast scoring game. It is best for two players, but two, three, or four can play. The game is played the same as the Five-up game with four variations.

Certain dominoes only may be set, and when a player plays a double or takes a score he plays again. These special features result in a concentrated burst of activity.

There are 1,184,040 possible hands, and the odds are different than in the Five-up game.

The hand:	Each player draws seven dominoes.
The set:	1. The set *must* be a double or a scoring domino.
	2. In a two- and three-handed game, if the setter cannot set a double or a scoring domino, he *must* draw from the boneyard; in a four-handed game, the setter passes.
The plays:	1. When a player, including the one on set, plays a double or scores, he *must* play again and again until he fails to score.
	2. After the set, the player may play any playable domino in his hand. If he plays a double or scores, and cannot make another play, in a two- or three-handed game he *must* draw from the boneyard until he secures a playable domino; in a four-handed game he passes.
	3. Players who previously passed play in turn or pass.
The last domino played:	A player cannot go out if his last play is a double or a score. If the last domino played will score, it must be played to score. If the player cannot go out, he must draw from the boneyard until he can play. If he is unable to play or draw, he passes until he can play in turn. Play continues until a player goes out without scoring or playing a double on his last play.

FORTY-TWO

CARD-TYPE BIDDING GAME

In this game no lines are built. The dominoes are played as cards in a card game. The game of Forty-two is a four-handed partnership game. Each player draws seven dominoes and all twenty-eight dominoes are in the players' hands. The game is played through hands of seven tricks each until one team makes the necessary 250 points to win. The players bid for each hand and the highest bidder names the trumps and leads.

This is a game of real skill in bidding and playing. There are 1,184,040 possible hands, and a player will rarely hold two hands that are the same.

Tricks and honors: Tricks and honors are what count.

Tricks—There are seven tricks and each counts 1 point.

Honors—Points are given for honor dominoes as follows:

6-4—10 points	5-0—5 points	3-2—5 points
5-5—10 points	4-1—5 points	

(The honor points go to the players who take the tricks.)

This makes a total of 42 possible points for each hand which gives the game its name.

Trumps: The trumps may be any one of the seven suits: 6, 5, 4, 3, 2, 1, or blank. The double of the trump bid is the highest, as, for example, if 3's are trump, the 3-3 is the highest, then the 3-6, 3-5, 3-4, 3-2, 3-1, and 3-0 in that order.

Doubles may be bid and when made trump, the highest double takes the trick.

No-trumps may also be bid as in bridge. In playing no-trump, the highest number of the piece led becomes the trump for that particular trick, and the other players must follow that trump or discard. In no-trump, the double is always the highest.

Partners and dealer: Players arrange or draw for partners and dealer. The dealer shuffles the dominoes and the players to his left, each in turn, draw seven dominoes. The deal rotates to the left.

Bidding: Bidding starts to the left of the dealer and rotates to the left. Each bidder bids the value of his hand and the other players may raise or pass, as they choose. Thirty is the lowest bid that can be made to start. If there is no bid, the deal rotates and new hands are drawn.

When a player has bid a limit bid, namely 42, each of the other players has the privilege of continuing the bid by doubling. After a bid of 42 is made, the next bidder must bid 84 or pass. The third bidder must bid 168 or pass, and the fourth bidder must bid 250 or pass. Bidding is continued until one player secures the bid after all others have passed. (Bids above 42 are made only by taking all 42 points.)

Trumps are not named until the bidding is completed.

Play: Highest bidder makes the opening lead and must play a trump. A nontrump lead calls the higher number on the domino the controlling suit. Each player must follow suit. If he cannot do so, he can either trump or discard. The player who takes the trick leads on the next round of the hand. The object is to win the counters (honor dominoes) and all tricks.

Score: There are two ways of scoring:

1. Most players score the hand according to whether or not the bidder made his bid. They simply *use a mark for each hand* won or lost, until the predetermined number of marks have been won by one team. Five marks may be used for a 250-point game, letting each mark be worth 50 points. Fast players use 10 marks, each worth 25 points.

2. Some players *score points.* Each team scores the number of points taken in. One point is counted for each trick and 5 or 10 points for each honor domino according to its value. When limit bids (including those doubled) have been made, the winner counts the amount of his bid. If the bidder fails to make his bid, the opponents score the amount of his bid plus the points that they make.

Game:

1. The game is 250 points.

2. The team that reaches 250 points or more at the finish of any hand wins the game. If both teams reach 250 points or more, the team that is ahead wins.

3. The last hand must be played out.

Individual scores: At domino parties each player's score is kept individually and prizes are given as at bridge and whist games.

LATIN-AMERICAN "DOMINO"

A SEVEN-DRAW
PARTNERSHIP BLOCK GAME
AND VARIATIONS FOR 2, 3, OR 4

This game is played extensively in Latin-American and some European countries. It is one of the various "block" games played on the principle of matching or following suit in a line. The object is to "block" the game, so that no one can play, or to domino (go out) by getting rid of all the dominoes in your hand and score the count in the opponents' hands. A score is made only at the end of each hand.

Two, three, or four may play. Four may play individually or as partners. Partners are chosen either by draw or agreement.

The Play

The dominoes are placed on the table face down and shuffled. Each player draws seven dominoes. At the start the player who holds the 6-6 is automatically "on set" and plays it. In the two- and three-handed games the player with the highest double sets. The turn to play rotates. (In Latin and South American countries they rotate to the right, counterclockwise.) After the set each domino must be played to a matching domino. Plays can be made once on either end of a singles domino and on both sides of a double, but not on the ends of a double. Singles must be played end to end. Doubles must cross singles.

If a player cannot play in turn, he passes. The other players continue to play until such time as he is able to play in turn, or until no one can play and the game becomes blocked. (In two- and three-handed games, the players may agree in advance that a player who is unable to play must draw from the boneyard until he draws one that will play, but the last two may not be drawn in a two-handed game and the last one in a three-handed game. If a player does not draw a playable domino he passes.) The rules on misplays are the same as in the Five-up game.

The hand is at an end when one of the players gets rid of all his dominoes. The player who goes out calls "domino," and the player or team receives the count of the dominoes in the opponents' hands. One point is counted for each spot.

If each of the players has one or more dominoes, but is unable to play to any one of them, the hand is "blocked." If the game is blocked, all of the players turn their dominoes face up and count the spots on the dominoes remaining in their hands. The team with the lowest count receives all the points in the opponents' hands. In the event of a tie there is no score.

After the first hand the player or team that won the previous hand sets. Any piece (double or single) may be set. In the four-handed partnership game either partner may set. They look at their dominoes and decide between themselves who shall set. Each new game is started by the player who holds the 6-6 (or the highest double in the two- and three-handed games).

The Points

Game is 100 or 150 points. The players usually play for a fixed amount for each game. Some play for the difference between the scores and game, as 1 unit for each point and 10 for game. In addition, the following penalties may also be added:

Player unable to play—four-handed—individual play

If one or more players are unable to play, they pay an agreed penalty to the player who made the last play. This is in addition to the amount for the game. The game continues until one player dominoes or the game is blocked.

Double for skunks—two-, three-, or four-handed

In individual or team play, if a player or team has not scored during the entire game, it is considered a "skunk" and the player or team that was "skunked" must pay double the amount for the game.

The Strategy

In this game there are 1,184,040 possible hands. The possibility of a player getting two hands that are alike is very remote. The skill is in playing each hand. The strategy is to block (close) the game if you are certain the count left in your team's hands is less than that of your opponents', or to domino. There are five fundamentals:

1. Set the longest suit.
   Set the double of your longest suit. Exception: If you hold five of one suit, including the double, and three of another suit, set the singles domino with both numbers. In this event you should put up the number of your long suit as soon as possible and keep the double until there is no play at the other end. If you do not have three or more of one suit, including the double, let your partner have the set. (Some good players will let their partner set if they consider their partner a weak player on the "theory" they can help their partner.)

2. Keep your team solvent.
   There can never be more than two numbers open in this game. After the set there are only two possible things that can be done:
   (a) Play a singles domino on a single number or off of the sides of a double. This cuts off the number played on, whether it is a single or a double (when one side of the double has already been played on) and it puts up a new number or one that is the same as the other end.
   (b) Play a double on a single number. This leaves the open ends unchanged.

The choice of playing a singles domino or a double depends upon whether you want to cut off a number, put up a new one, or leave the numbers unchanged.

If your partner is on set, the second time he plays his chance of playing is approximately 95 times out of 100 if there are two numbers open and approximately 80 times out of 100 if there is only one number open. On your first play it is important for you to get him two numbers to play on, if possible. If he set a double, play a double on the second player's number, if possible; otherwise, play a singles on it. Leave your partner's double alone. If your partner set a singles, cross his number with a double, if possible, or play a singles on the second player's number or play a double on it if necessary. With this play the odds will be in favor of your partner (setter) having two numbers to play on. Watch your partner's plays and help him, if possible. Put up his numbers, play new or lead-back numbers, and play doubles on his numbers and lead-back numbers. Get him two numbers to play on, if possible. If you can block the game and assure your winning the hand you may, of course, take over and play to win.

If you are on set, get the line back to your long suit or suits as often as possible. Force two numbers up that you can play on, if possible, and get rid of your doubles. When you hold several doubles, try to play, first, those of the same number being played by your opponents, and second, those being played by your partner.

There is only one way the game can be blocked (closed). This can be done only when five dominoes of a particular number, excluding the double (whether played or not), have been played and the player holds the sixth singles domino of that number. He can block the game *only* if he is given the remaining lead-back number to that suit. The game is blocked by singles and not the double, even though the double may be the final play.

See Part 5, "How to Master Suit Control." This explains how the lead-back numbers work and the playback technique. This is the one big thing to learn. Also, see Part 4, "How to Evaluate Specific Plays." During the play you should have gained valuable information. This shows you how to interpret your partner's and opponents' plays.

3. Block your opponents.

If your opponents are on set, block the player on set, if possible, forcing him to pass and go off set. This puts your team in a position to domino.

When you are the fourth player, on your first play you should play on your opponent's set and put up the same number as the other end, if possible. In this way you leave the setter only one number to play on. If you have to put up a new number you at least cut off his original number. As a general rule, cut off your opponents' numbers and lead-back numbers. Put up your team's numbers or a double if you want to avoid giving your opponent a new number.

If your opponents are on set, as a general rule, postpone playing the doubles, as they have no value in blocking the game. However, when the fifth domino of a number is played you must play your double, unless you also hold the seventh domino of that number. Otherwise your double may be cut off and made an orphan.

Before blocking the game so no one can play, you should definitely determine that the total score of the dominoes in your opponents' hands is more than that in your team's hands. This can be estimated by the pieces played, the numbers your opponents and your partner have been playing and those in your hand.

4. Play favorable percentage.

The chances of any one other player (1, 2, or 3) holding *one particular number* after you look at your hand depends upon how many you hold. The chances of the other player holding one or more is 83 out of 100 if you hold three, 73 out of 100 if you hold four, 57 out of 100 if you hold five, and 33 out of 100 if you hold six.

After the hand is started, these odds will change, but not radically, until one or more of that particular number has been played. For method of determining the chances of any other player holding a particular number or a particular domino see Part 6, "Making Your Choice of Plays."

5. Get rid of your large dominoes.

This is good defense. If large numbers are set or played, the count remaining in the hands will be small; if small numbers are set or played, the count remaining in the hands will be large.

BLOCK

A SIMPLE MATCHING GAME

The Block game is the simplest of all domino games. Two, three, or four may play. The players may play individually or as partners. With two, each player draws seven dominoes for his hand. With three or four, each takes five dominoes.

The players draw for set. The rules for starting the game are the same as for Five-up. See pages 9, 10, on "Shuffle and Set" and "Drawing Hand" and "Boneyard."

Object

A score is made only at the end of each hand. The object is to get rid of all the dominoes in your hand. Your plan is to block the other player so that he cannot make a play. A good player will put up a number he has in his hand, especially if he has three or more. If you can get up two numbers you have in your hand you are sure of another play. Your aim is to get the line back to your numbers as often as possible.

Play

Any domino may be set.

After the set each domino must be played to a matching domino. Doubles must cross singles. Singles must be played end to end.

Plays can be made once on either end of a singles domino and on both sides of a double but not on the ends of a double.

If a player cannot play in turn, he passes. He may not draw from the boneyard. The other players continue to play until such time as he is able to play in turn, or until no one can play and the game becomes blocked.

Points

The hand is at an end when one of the players gets rid of all his dominoes. The player who goes out calls "domino." He receives all the count in the other players' or team's hands. One point is counted for each spot, a count of 15 being 15 points.

If each of the players has one or more dominoes, but is unable to play to any of them, the hand is "blocked." If the game is blocked, all of the players turn their dominoes face up and count the spots on the dominoes remaining in their hands. The player or team with the lowest count receives all the points in the opponents' hands. In the event of a tie there is no score.

Game is 61 points, or 100 or 150 if preferred.

Optional Rules

1. Drawing from boneyard.

A player having no playable domino may be required to draw from the boneyard until he gets one that will play, but the last two may not be drawn in a two-handed game and the last one in a three- or four-handed game. If a player does not draw a playable domino, he passes.

2. Continuing to play.

A variation of the four-handed partnership game is for each to play for himself, but instead of playing one domino at a time in each round, a player may go on as long as he can follow suit to either end of the line.

SEBASTOPOL

A DIFFERENT BLOCK GAME

Sebastopol is a "block" game, but it is different from all the others. It is a four-handed game. Each player draws seven dominoes and plays individually. All of the twenty-eight dominoes are in the players' hands. A score is made only at the end of each hand.

Play

The player who holds the 6-6 is automatically "on set" and plays it.

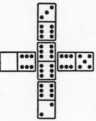

The turn to play rotates to the left (clockwise), and each player must play a 6 to the 6-6. Nothing but 6's can be played until both sides and both ends of the 6-6 have been covered. If a player cannot play, he must pass.

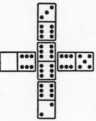

When four dominoes have been played on the 6-6, any of the four ends may be played on. Players can then play a double or a singles. Further plays on doubles may be made on the sides but not on the ends of doubles. Each player in turn must play or pass.

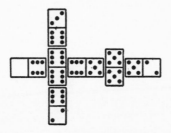

Points

The player who goes out on the hand scores the count in the other players' hands. If the game is blocked, the player with the lowest count receives all the points in the opponents' hands. In the event of a tie, there is no score.

Game is 61 points.

MUGGINS

A SIMPLE SCORING GAME

Muggins is a simple matching and scoring game. Scores are made in two ways—first, by making the total count of the ends played on the table total 5 or a multiple of 5 and, second, by the total count of the dominoes remaining in the opponents' hands after one of the players goes out by being the first to get rid of all of his dominoes.

Two, three, or four may play. Four may play individually or as partners. With two, each player draws seven dominoes for his hand. With three or four, each takes five.

Object

The main object is to score during play and, secondarily, to get rid of all the dominoes in your hand. If a player has no playable domino in his hand, he is forced to draw from the boneyard. Your plan is to put up a number you have in your hand, especially if you have two or more. In a two-handed game, if you can get up two numbers you have in your hand, you are sure of another play. This keeps you able to play and may force your opponent to the boneyard. If you are playing a partnership game and your partner is on set, your strategy is to help your partner go out. The way to do this is to play a double on his number, put up his number at the first opportunity, or play a number that leads back to his number.

Draw and Set

The players draw for set. The rules for starting the game are the same as in Five-up. See pages 9, 10, on "Shuffle and Set," "Drawing Hand," and "Boneyard."

Play

Any domino may be set. Plays on a single may be made once only off of each end.

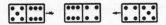

A double must be played crosswise, and both its ends count in the total until it is canceled by the play of another domino on it. Plays on doubles may be made on both sides but not on the ends of the doubles.

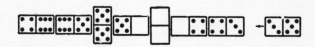

Drawing from Boneyard

A player having no playable domino must draw from the boneyard until he gets one that will play, but the last two may not be drawn in a two-handed game and the last one in a three- or four-handed game. If the player does not draw a playable domino, he passes.

Points

When the total count of the open ends totals 5 or a multiple of 5, the player (or team) that makes the combination receives 5 points for each multiple of 5 on the table. All spots on a double are counted, but only when it is an end. Doubles that have been played on both sides are not counted.

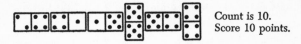

Count is 10.
Score 10 points.

The player (or team) who plays his last domino first goes out on the hand and receives 5 points for each multiple of 5 in the opponents' hands. A remainder of 3 or 4 count as 5, those of 1 or 2 as nothing.

If each of the players have one or more dominoes, but are unable to play any one of them or draw from the boneyard, the hand is "closed." The player (or team) having the lowest count receives the score in the opponents' hands. If the lowest count is tied, there is no score.

Game is 61 points. The game is finished at the end of the hand
that a player (or team) makes 61 points or more. If both players
make game, the one that is ahead wins. In case of a tie, two more
hands must be played.

Optional Rules

1. Plays may be made on the ends of the *first double* as well
as the sides, giving four plays off of the first double. With this
rule there may be two, three, or four open ends in the layout.

2. Scoring may be done on the basis of one point for each
multiple of 5. This rule is usually applied when plays are made
off of the first double.

BERGEN

A DIFFERENT SCORING GAME

Bergen is a "scoring" game, but it is different from the simple
Muggins and popular Five-up games. Two, three, or four can
play. Each player draws six dominoes and plays individually. The
object of the game is to make the numbers at the two ends of the
line alike. When a player does this, it is called a double-header.
When one of the two ends is a double, it becomes a triple-header.

Draw and Set: The players draw for set. The rules for starting the
game are the same as for Five-up. See pages 9, 10, on "Shuffle
and Set," "Drawing Hand," and "Boneyard."

Play: Each play must match the open end on which the domino is
played. Singles are played end to end. A double must cross the
single. Plays on a double may be made only on the sides of the
double but not on the ends of the double.

Scoring: When a double is set, it scores 2 points. A player making
the ends of the line alike scores 2 points. If there is a double at
one end, and a singles of the same number can be played at
the other end, or if a double can be added to one end of a
double-header, it makes a triple-header and scores 3 points.
The player who plays his last domino first goes out and scores
1 point.

Drawing from boneyard: When a player cannot follow suit, he
must draw from the boneyard until he gets a domino that can
be played, but the last two in the boneyard may not be drawn.

Blocked game: If the players are blocked, the dominoes in the hand are shown and the player having the smallest count wins 1 point. However, if the lowest holds a double and his opponent has none, the opponent wins. If two have doubles and one has none, the player with none wins. If there is a double in each hand, the lowest double wins. If there is more than one double in anyone's hand and all have doubles, the one with the least number of doubles wins without reference to the size of the double.

Game: The game is 15 points.

DOMINO POOL

A PARTY GAME FOR THREE TO SIX PERSONS

This is an excellent party game that makes for a lot of fun. It is easy to learn and anyone can play it. Any number from three to six persons can play. Each hand a pool is made up by the players putting in an agreed amount of chips. The pool goes to the winner of the hand. A prize may be given to the player with the most chips.

Object: This is a "block" game. There is no scoring. The object is to go out on the hand first. The player who goes out wins the pool.

The strategy is to select a domino of your longest suit, especially if you have three or more, and endeavor to get the line back to your suit as often as possible. Your secondary objective is to block your opponents so that they cannot follow suit or make a play.

Draw and set: Players draw for set. The rules for starting the game are the same as for Five-up. See pages 9, 10, on "Shuffle and Set," "Drawing Hand," and "Boneyard."

Original draw: The draw varies with the number of players. Each player takes such a number of dominoes as will leave at least eight dominoes in the boneyard.

Play: The player on set can play any domino and each following player must follow suit if he can, to one end or the other. A double may be played but must cross the single. A single played on a double must be played off of either side of the double, but not on the ends of the double. If a person cannot play he "passes," and the player on his left plays or passes also.

Drawing from boneyard: The play can be varied by requiring the player who is unable to play to draw from the boneyard until he gets one that will play. All of the dominoes in the boneyard, with the exception of one, may be drawn.

Closed game: If all players are blocked, the one with the smallest count left in his hand wins; ties divide.

PART 10

Glossary

Domino Terms and Players' Jargon

AROUND THE CORNER—A score beyond the halfway point in the game that places the team's position in the last half of the scoreboard. Team is beyond the halfway mark and may not be skunked.

BANKER'S SET —Humorous name for the 3-2 set. It scores and is the only domino that cannot be scored on by the next player.

BLEEDING —A player, particularly the one on set, who is unable to play off of a single number and must play off of a double, usually his own, thus indicating he is short of numbers and probably in trouble.

BLOCK —To cut off a number and prevent the next player from playing on that particular number or from playing on any number.

BLOCK GAMES —Games in which the objective is to prevent the opponent from playing.

BOARD —The scoreboard and round pegs used to record the scores made by the players.

BONES —The twenty-eight domino pieces.

BOOB SET —Humorous name for the 4-1 set, insinuating it was played solely for the sake of 1 point.

BONEYARD —The dominoes remaining in the deck after the players have drawn their hands.

BOXCARS —The 6-6. The two 6's end to end resemble two freight cars of a train.

CARD GAMES —Card games adapted to dominoes.

CROSS —Playing a double domino on a single number. Also, playing a singles off of a double to form a cross or a "T," as 6-3 off of the 6-6.

CUT IN —To take turns in playing when five or more persons desire to play in a four-handed game.

CUTTHROAT —A three-handed game in which each person plays for himself and against the other two. A name

derived from the practice of two opponents playing together to force the player on set to draw
and go off set. Similar to Igorotte except in the
method of scoring.

DANCING GIRLS   —Spirited scoring with 5's. All dominoes with a five
are "kickers" commonly called "dancing girls."

DOUBLE   —A domino with two numbers or two blanks that
are the same, such as the 5-5 or the 0-0.

DOUBLES AND   —6-6 Boxcars   3-3 Poison Ivy   0-0 Ivory Soap
THEIR NAMES   5-5 Gold   2-2 Pair of
             Nuggets   Ducks
           4-4 Scorpion   1-1 Snake Eyes

DOUBLES GAME   —A four-handed game with the players teamed up
as partners.

DRAW GAME   —Game with a rule that a player having no playable domino must draw from the boneyard until
he gets one that plays.

DUCKS, PAIR OF   —The 2-2. The two dots in each section are in right
echelon and resemble two ducks in flight.

ENDS   —Either number or section of a domino piece. The
extreme or last numbers in a line of dominoes
formed on the table.

FARMER'S SET   —Humorous name for the 6-4 set insinuating it was
played solely for the sake of the 2 points.

FOLLOWING DOMINO—A domino that repeats a previous score.

GO   —Used in block games to signify player is unable
to play.

GOLD NUGGETS   —The 5-5. The 5-5 in a player's hand is worth its
weight in gold like two gold nuggets.

GO OUT   —To end the play in a particular hand. The first
player to play all of the dominoes in his hand
goes out. Also called "to domino."

HAIRY BELLY   —Humorous name for the 6-6.

HIT THE DECK   —Player has no domino in hand which will play—
forced to draw from the deck.

IDIOT'S DELIGHT   —Humorous name for the 5-0 set insinuating it was
set solely for the sake of 1 point.

IGORROTE   —A three-handed domino game in which each person plays for himself and against the other two.

A name derived from a tribe of headhunters, the Igorrotes. Similar to "Cutthroat" except in the method of scoring.

IVORY SOAP —The 0-0. The double blank resembles a bar of white soap.

KIBITZER —A person who is permitted to stand or sit around a game and observe its progress. Some are prone to make various kinds of noises during the play of the hand. These sounds run the gamut from clucking, sighing, gasping, and wheezing to comments, inaudible to audible, which in many cases are leading and informatory. Such offenders are subject to serious reprimand, censure, battery, or mayhem.

KICKER —A domino that will score 1 point more than the previous play. All dominoes with a 5 and the 6-1. The 6-5, 4-5, 3-5, 2-5, 1-5, and 0-5 played off of a spinner will add 5 to the count and score 1 point more than the previous play. The 5-5 will increase a previous score 1 point when played on a 5.

LAYOUT —The dominoes that have been played on the table in a matching game.

LEAD —The first play made by the player on set. Also, the player who takes control and directs the play for his team.

LEAD-BACK NUMBER—A number that leads to a play with a particular domino of a particular suit. The lead-back number and the suit number are identical.

LIGHTHOUSE —A double in a player's hand without any matching numbers. A lighthouse played on the first play of a hand is a "lighthouse set."

LIQUID —Keeping the play open so that the player can follow with a play.

LOW RENT DISTRICT—Score beyond the halfway point, avoiding a skunk.

MAKE THE DOMINOES —To shuffle or mix the dominoes thoroughly before the players draw their hands. This is done by the players to the left of the player on set. Also referred to as "Make."

MAN OVERBOARD —Player has no domino in hand that will play—forced to draw from the boneyard.

MINUS SET —A hand where the team on set scored less points on the hand than their opponents.

NEW LEADER —When the team or player who has been behind on points scores and goes ahead.

OFF SET —A player in first position to domino and go out who is forced to draw and thus go off of set position.

ON SET —Player who is in first position to go out in the hand being played.

ON THE BOARD —First score made by a team or player.

ORPHAN —The seventh domino of a particular number remaining in a player's hand and that cannot be played as all matching numbers have been covered.

OVERDRAW —To draw more than the prescribed number of dominoes in the original hand, or to draw from the boneyard when the player has a playable domino in his hand, in which event a penalty is applied.

PASS —Signifies player is unable to play, as he has no playable domino and he is unable to draw.

PASS THE DOMINOES—A player unable to play and required to draw from the deck requests that the dominoes remaining in the boneyard be moved in front of him for more convenient drawing.

PEG —The marker or pin used to record the score. "To peg" means to score.

PIGEON —A player who is easily beaten—an inexperienced player.

PILE —See "Boneyard."

PIP —A spot on a domino.

PLAYBACK —A play that puts up a lead-back number to a particular suit through a suit number that has not been played. It provides a play with the matching domino of the suit. Also, a play that puts up a number that provides the next player a play with a domino that will score.

PLUS SET —A hand where the team on set scored more points on the hand than their opponents.

POISON IVY —The 3-3. The three dots in each unit climb upward like poison ivy having glossy leaves of three leaflets.

PRESIDENT —Player in first position to go out.

PUSH —Count remaining in two players' hands is equal and neither receives a score.

REPEATER —A domino that will take the same score as was taken by the previous player.

SCORING GAME —Games with scoring in the course of play.

SCORING SETS AND THEIR HUMOROUS NAMES

6-4 Farmer's Set	5-0 Idiot's Delight	3-2 Banker's Set
5-5 Gold Nuggets	4-1 Boob Set	

SCORPION —The 4-4. The double 4 totals eight. The eighth sign of the Zodiac is Scorpio. The scorpion has eight legs.

SECOND SET —Player who holds the second position, to go out.

SET —The opening play of the hand. The first domino played after the hands have been drawn.

SINGLES DOMINO —A domino with two separate numbers or blank such as 0-5, 6-3.

SINGLES GAME —A game played by two players. A two-handed game. Also a four-handed game played individually.

SKUNK —A completed game in which the winning team or player scored 61 points or more and the losing team or player scored less than 31 points. The losing player is said to have been "skunked." An agreed penalty is usually applied.

SMELL SOMETHING —A possible skunk coming up.

SNAKE EYES —The 1-1. The two dots resemble the eyes of a snake.

SOLVENT —Player is in position to continue play and go out.

SPINNER —A double domino, as a 2-2 or 1-1, which has been played on two sides, thus providing two more plays off of each end.

SPOTS —The dots on the dominoes representing numbers.

STICKY HAND —A poor hand with little playing or scoring possibilities.

STINKER —A player who cuts off an opponent's number and sends him to the boneyard.

STINK HOLE   —A peg or marker in the last hole of either side of a scoreboard; score of 30 or 60. Used particularly when one team is about to "go out" and the other team has 30 points, thus in jeopardy of being "skunked."

STONES   —The twenty-eight domino pieces.

SUITS   —The dominoes with the same number. All the dominoes with the same number upon either end belong to the same suit; the seven pieces with a 2 form the 2 suit; those with a 6 the 6 suit, and so on.

TILE   —One of the twenty-eight domino pieces.

TO DOMINO   —The first player to dispose of all the dominoes in his hand goes out or dominoes.

VICE-PRESIDENT   —Player who is in second position to go out after his partner who is in first position.

WIRED   —A player who holds in his hand one or more dominoes that can be played off of one or more dominoes on the table and cannot be cut off by the opponent. Usually the player on set who cannot be prevented from going out.

Index and Tables of Player's Chances in Five-up Game

DRAWING
(ORIGINAL FIVE DOMINOES)

193

HOLDING
(ORIGINAL FIVE DOMINOES DRAWN)

DRAWING FROM BONEYARD